*"These things I have spoken to you,
That my joy may be in you,
and that your joy may be full."*

THE NIGHT
HE WAS
BETRAYED

*Bible Studies in our Lord's
preparation for his passion.*

by R. E. O. WHITE

WILLIAM B. EERDMANS PUBLISHING COMPANY
GRAND RAPIDS, MICHIGAN

Copyright © 1982 by William B. Eerdmans Publishing Co.
255 Jefferson Ave. S.E., Grand Rapids, MI 49503

Library of Congress Cataloging in Publication Data

White, R. E. O. (Reginald Ernest Oscar), 1914-
    The night he was betrayed.

    1. Bible. N.T. John XIII-XVII — Criticism, interpre-
tation, etc. I. Title.
BS2615.2.W49 1982   226'.507   82-13783
ISBN 0-8028-1942-7

Contents

Preface

OVER fifty years ago, a young lad newly converted sat alone on a sea wall on a lovely summer's day, alternately gazing across the rolling water and reading in snatches a thin, green paper-bound pamphlet entitled "The Three Full Assurances." Most of the contents are long forgotten, together with the author's name, but not the experience that there came to a groping, immature, timid Christian heart, a quickening of mind, a surge of joy, a sense of the presence and love of God almost unparalleled in half a century. There was born the first sense of the power within Scripture, and the depth of Christian truth: that, too, has never been forgotten.

The lad has often wanted to repay that debt by attempting to write something similar, a straightforward exposition of some part of Scripture, so unfolding its meaning and its application to Christian life as to move other hearts to similar gladness and wonder.

Whether the following Bible study succeeds to the faintest degree in that purpose, only the occasional reader will know. But that at least is the intention which prompted discovery and sharing of the rich vein of Christian truth within some of the profoundest words ever uttered. Few passages of Scripture are more precious than the table-talk of Jesus in the upper room in Jerusalem on that night on which he was betrayed. As the Master himself said, "These things I have spoken to you, that my joy may be in you, and that your joy may be full."

THE NIGHT HE
WAS BETRAYED

1:
For Them and Us

THAT memorable conversation of Jesus with his men, in the upper room in Jerusalem on the night before he died, has supreme importance for all time.

The words there spoken are extraordinarily impressive, solemn, searching, instructive. Some of them, like the parable of the vine ("Let not your hearts be troubled . . . ," the promise of the Spirit), are exceedingly important, and have endeared themselves to Christian hearts. That all which was done, said, and prayed in that upper room took place around and across the Lord's table only intensifies the interest and reverence of this final self-disclosure of Jesus to the inner circle of his disciples just before his passion.

In any case, the conversation of that evening has by some means been recorded, and at length, for our instruction — like the "private" conversations with Nicodemus and the woman in Samaria. It is a primary principle governing all understanding of the Gospels that the writers were not concerned merely to record what Jesus said and did; they were at least equally concerned to show the relevance of what he said and did for the faith and experience of their readers. When John pauses to underline the significance of what he has said — "*we* have beheld his glory"; "He who saw it has borne witness . . . that you also may believe" (1:14, 16; 19:35, see also 11:51; 20:31) — this "two-timing" of the story is especially clear.

That is why the four Gospels differ in their selection, arrangement, and emphasis, while telling essentially the same story. Each writer has in mind the spiritual condition and need of the church he knows as he decides what to recall of Christ's teaching and example and how to present it. John certainly intended the church of his own time (probably toward the end of the first century) to overhear and to heed what Jesus had to say. It was spoken for them, too.

In one respect, Christ's words on that occasion were directed

3

even more to the church that was to be than to those immediately present. His main theme was "the time between the advents": the circumstances, needs, dangers, and resources of the days between his "going" and his "coming again." He spoke of work and peril in the wider world beyond the hills of Galilee and the crowded streets of Jerusalem. If the Eleven needed instruction as they looked forward fearfully to that time, so did the church of John's day, who lived in the midst of it. And so do we, who still look backwards and forwards, in remembrance and hope.

This is dramatically underlined when suddenly we find *ourselves* mentioned in the prayer that closes the evening: "I do not pray for these only," says Jesus, "but also for them who are to believe in me through their word." Into the compass of that sentence, and so into the intercession of Jesus so long ago, are drawn all the generations of Christians, of many lands and many types, who have inherited the apostolic testimony and have believed in Christ.

Because we were not among the privileged guests, we must not presume to understand perfectly all that took place in the upper room, but we must acknowledge with reverence that some things about the record puzzle us, and some seem impossible to explain with assurance. Not being present, we miss inflections, glances, and nuances that might illumine all; imagination may help to fill gaps and suggest connections, but imagination must be reverent, and extremely cautious, if it desires the truth.

For examples, we know that there had been contention that day among the disciples. We know, too, that in that upper room that evening Jesus took bread and broke it, poured wine and shared it, and spoke the memorable words that set the Lord's table at the center of Christian worship in all generations. Yet John does not mention either fact. His record, then, is incomplete. We may speculate upon why this is so, but we must not pretend to know.

Again, we are surprised that so long a discourse, and especially the intense and prolonged prayer that follows it, should have been recorded at all. Did someone take notes? Is it a remarkable feat of memory? Or should we think simply of miracle — of the Holy Spirit's bringing to remembrance the things that Christ uttered? This "explanation" would seem to be what John implies. Sometimes we can trace the ways in which the

Spirit preserved the story — by oft-repeated patterns of oral teaching, by numerous attempts at summarizing events (as Luke tells Theophilus), by the use of source documents, and the like. The aids to John's inspired memories and occasional interpretation are harder to discern: we must be content to interpret the record as it stands, though we shall wonder, sometimes, if the emphasis and application do not also reflect the church's later experience.

There are some other puzzles. Every careful reader notices the injunction at the end of chapter 14: "Rise, let us go hence." Some translations attempt to disguise that meaning, which is certainly what the original says. Yet there follow the parable of the true vine, which has no obvious connection with chapter 14, and two whole chapters of further teaching, and one of prayer, before John tells us, "When Jesus had spoken these words, he went forth" (18:1).

Imagination has been busy at explanation, suggesting further talk and prayer as the group makes its way through the streets (contradicting 18:1); interpreting the words as a final resolve to meet the "ruler of this world"; or hearing in them the decision to go to the Father. Such speculation is permissible, but scarcely persuasive. As the record stands, Jesus did not "go" anywhere, but went on talking; 14:31 remains a puzzle.

But so does 16:5 — "Now I am going to him who sent me; yet none of you asks me, ' "Where are you going?" " For Peter had earlier asked precisely that, in 13:36 — "Simon Peter said to him, 'Lord, where are you going?' " Thomas, too, had remarked in 14:5, "Lord, we do not know where you are going. . . ." As Jesus' words are now given, they sound strangely like an undeserved rebuke.

It is odd, too, to hear Jesus say "Let not your hearts be troubled . . ." immediately following the warning to Peter that he would three times deny that he knew Jesus. That *cannot* mean that denying Jesus need not spoil our peace!

This occasional impression that the narrative is disconnected is greatly strengthened when we notice how repetitious these chapters are. The thought appears, sometimes, to circle around a few themes that recur once and again. For example, the coming of the Spirit is introduced into the discussion in chapter 14, dropped throughout 15, and taken up again in 16.

5

The relation of servant and master occurs in chapter 13 and again in 15. Christ's going away is discussed in chapters 13, 14, not in 15, but recurs in 16. So with words about prayer, introduced in chapter 14, occurring again in 15 and 16. And the legacy of peace, spoken of in chapter 14, is repeated in 16.

There are in fact fifteen, or perhaps seventeen, examples of this doubling back upon what has already been said, giving to the superficial reader an impression of rambling, almost desultory, talk, rather than of purposeful discussion of topics in due order. Because of this repetitive structure, the best method of study at some points is not by pursuing straight through, inventing connections of thought that are not there, but by taking up what Jesus said, on this theme and on that, scattered through the chapters as we now have them.

Explanation of these features of the discourse — apparent contradictions, disconnectedness, repetition — is another matter. Again imagination has been busy. Some would rearrange paragraphs to straighten out the conversation. Some even transfer parts of the discourse to the days following Christ's resurrection. It has been noticed that if we tabulate the fifteen (or seventeen?) topics on which Jesus appears to speak twice or three times, the first mention is always in chapters 13 or 14, and the repetition is in chapters 15 or 16. The references fall on *either side of that puzzling 14:31.*

This is intriguing. It suggests that John *may* have had available two separate accounts of what happened in the upper room. One (supposedly) told of the washing of the disciples' feet, the comment and conversation that followed, and the injunction to rise and go hence, immediately obeyed as the group departed to cross the Kidron to Gethsemane. The alternative account told of the parable of the true vine, promises concerning the Spirit, and Jesus' prayer for his own. Two such accounts would naturally overlap. Wishing to lose nothing, perhaps John set both down, necessarily one after the other, although they should be read simultaneously, so to speak, as parallel records of the same evening of talk.

It is important to realize that *all* such explanations are imaginative reconstructions of what might have happened. Each Bible student chooses the explanation that happens to appeal to him or her the most. No one may be dogmatic, since evidence is lacking.

Nor do theories greatly concern us in the attempt to discover the truth that John believed Jesus unveiled in the upper room, and that the church in John's own day needed to hear again. The puzzles in the record remind us that we are eavesdroppers in the upper room, not guests, and they warn us not to be deceived by the simplicity of the language into thinking the meaning obvious and the teaching elementary. John 13–17 is certainly one of the richest passages in all Scripture. From one point of view, we need to stand upon our mental watchtower to hear what Christ the Lord would say to us, neither distorting, nor simplifying, nor evading things harder to understand. From another point of view, we need to take our shoes from off our feet, for the place whereon we stand is holy ground, leading directly up to Calvary.

Sitting often at the Lord's table, have I ever given a thought to what Jesus had to say across that hallowed board? Am I willing, even yet, to let him instruct and challenge, warn and reassure me, out of the gathering shadows in that distant upper room?

2:
The Right Approach

AN interpreter's assumptions are very important. We all approach Scripture with predetermined questions, to which we seek satisfactory answers, and with fairly settled opinions about the kind of teaching we ought to find there. And our "line of approach" to any passage, parable, story, or doctrine usually determines what we make of it. It is well, therefore, for interpreter and listener to be aware of what those assumptions are; and since opinions without reasons are merely prejudices, others should have the opportunity to judge for themselves whether our approach is reasonable and right.

To stand back from John 13–17 and consider it as a whole is to remember at once that it forms only part of a whole book, although a substantial part. Measured in chapters or in pages, this section is one quarter of John's Gospel. The "discourse" and prayer together are longer than Matthew's "sermon on the mount," a great deal longer than any other recorded utterance of Jesus.

John admits that his story is hopelessly incomplete:

> Jesus did many other signs in the presence of the disciples, which are not written in this book; . . . were every one of them to be written, I suppose that the world itself could not contain the books that would be written.
>
> (20:30; 21:25)

Yet, so pressed for space, John gives a quarter of what is available to this one evening's conversation. Plainly, the upper room marks far more than a quiet, intimate interlude. That familiar impression must be dispelled at once. These chapters represent an integral part of John's plan and an important stage in his great argument.

The impressive solemnity with which John introduces this long interview with the Twelve (13:1–3), and its position as virtually "replacing" the Lord's supper in his story, confirm the special significance that John saw in the occasion.

The Setting in John's Gospel

What John's argument was designed to show he tells us plainly:

> "These [signs] are written that you may believe that Jesus is the Christ, the Son of God, and that believing you may have life in his name."
>
> (20:31)

John's Gospel is thus a theological tract, arguing that Jesus is Messiah and Son of God, with evangelistic purpose — that we, the readers, may believe and find life in him.

To this end, John introduces Jesus in a series of testimonies — those of the Baptist, Andrew, Philip, Nathanael, and his own and that of the church around him: "We have beheld his glory . . . from his fullness have we all received. . . ." Then John presents a series of striking deeds, "signs" as John calls them, such as turning the water into wine, feeding five thousand from paltry resources, healing a man blind from birth, raising the dead. In each, Jesus "manifests forth his glory," illustrates some aspect of his mission, so that men and women come to believe on him.

With these deeds, John also presents Jesus' revealing words — about making known the God whom no man has seen, about new birth, about worship and the nature of God as spirit, about his own relation to the Father, about eternal life. Among these dramatic words are certain startling claims, such as "I AM Messiah, the bread of life, the light of the world, the resurrection and the life. . . ." These lead, on the one hand, to great controversy, and, on the other, to widening and deepening faith.

All the way through the Gospel, Jesus bears witness to "him who sent me," that others "may see" (9:38). The unforgettable climax to the whole story-argument comes when, against all probability, Thomas falls before the risen Jesus in adoring confession, "My Lord and my God!" Thereupon Jesus pronounces his final beatitude, "Have you believed because you have seen me? Blessed are those who have not seen and yet believe."

It is fair to summarize this close-knit argument as "Jesus manifesting himself, in deeds, words, claims and controversy, with a view to kindling life-giving faith." And it is essential to see chapters 13–17 as a vital part of that argument. Jesus continues to manifest himself with a view to faith, but now espe-

9

cially to that small group upon whom the future depends, and in the urgent, pressing situation of the night on which he was betrayed.

The opportunity has been very carefully planned. John does not tell (as Mark does, 14:12f.) how Jesus had previously arranged for a guide to this upper room, equipped with an agreed-upon password, or how he detached two of the disciples to go ahead and prepare, doing all in such a way that the rest — especially Judas — had no idea where the meal would take place. Instead, on a much wider canvas, John shows how this interview marked a deliberate and crucial change in Christ's whole strategy.

In the verses that lead up to chapters 13–17 John recalls how Jesus warned "the crowd":

> "The light is with you for a little longer. Walk while you have the light, lest the darkness overtake you. . . . While you have the light, believe in the light, that you may become sons of light." When Jesus had said this, *he departed and hid himself* from them.

The public ministry had ended: "Yet a little while and the world will see me no more" (14:19). John adds a comment on the crowd's unbelief, and then shows how Jesus, in turning from public to private "self-manifestation," strove to prepare the inner circle of disciples for the test of faith ahead of them. He strove to make himself, his mission, and his destiny more clearly understood. He had "yet many things to say" to them (16:12), and needed these few last private hours, undisturbed, to talk with his own, that they too might believe.

It follows that we must be prepared to find in these chapters not simply pious comfort and pleasant promises, but a far-reaching and important part of Christ's self-revelation about his own person and work, his vital "last words" before he died.

The Setting in the Gospels

John follows chapters 13–17 immediately with a detailed account of the arrest, trial, and death of Jesus, and his resurrection appearances. Such is the culmination of that whole movement of Christ from God into the world and out of the world back to the Father with which John opens chapter 13. In this way, 13–17 not only completes what went before, it constitutes also *John's introduction to the story of Christ's passion.*

To this extent, John follows the pattern of each of the Gospels, and not only in the obvious sense that every account of Jesus must wind to that conclusion. More importantly, each Gospel can be described as "a passion-story with introduction." From the space allotted to Jesus' trial and death, and to the teaching that prepares for it, it is clear that each Gospel-writer sees in the death of Jesus the real meaning of all else.

Matthew shows how the earlier teaching about the kingdom of God was replaced after Caesarea Philippi by teaching about the cross; and he leads up to that climax with some ten or eleven statements by Jesus that illumine the meaning of his death. Mark, too, records this change of emphasis in Christ's teaching, but he also analyzes fully the opposition Jesus faced, and includes the great utterance about giving his life a ransom for many, to explain why Jesus died.

Luke so emphasizes Christ's redeeming ministry, his words at Calvary (23:34, 42), and the fulfillment of Scripture (24:25–27) that we are left with no question why Jesus died. John, too, has said much in earlier chapters to point forward to Christ's death and to explain its meaning. Yet in the upper room the disciples are still bewildered and unprepared, perplexed and troubled by Jesus' talk of "going away": "Lord, where are you going?" . . . "Why cannot I follow you now?" . . . "Lord, we do not know where you are going" . . . "What is this that he says to us, 'A little while and you will not see me.' . . . We do not know what he means."

We are justified, therefore, in expecting that in this last talk with the Twelve immediately before his arrest, Jesus would seek once more to explain what lies ahead, and why. We should not assume that he will, but we will not be surprised to find it so.

A similar comparison with the other Gospels reveals a second striking parallel. All three recall that Jesus, just before his death, discussed at length with the disciples the program for the future. Each records what is usually described as "an eschatological discourse," a long farewell and forecast of "the last things."

Mark has one condensed chapter (13) foretelling the destruction of Jerusalem, "the End," suffering and declension, calling for great watchfulness. Matthew has two (or three) chapters (23–25) likewise giving the "signs of the end" and of the "coming of the son of man," but adding three priceless parables of the future. Luke summarizes all into one chapter (21).

At first sight, John omits everything of this kind. He has nothing about the fall of Jerusalem, darkened skies, wars and rumors of wars, or Christ coming on the clouds; no parables of bridesmaids, talents, fig trees, or sheep and goats. Nor, in John, does Jesus bid faithful servants to watch: he says, "no longer do I call you servants" (15:15).

Nevertheless, Jesus' last discourse in John, too, shows the same preoccupation with the future, the same confidence concerning his own place within it. Here, too, Jesus speaks of the judgment of this world, of his own victory, of his presence among believers to the end of the age, of his "coming." All sounds different, yet essentially the same notes of "eschatological" hope are struck. Jesus goes to prepare a place, and will return for his own. Again, he will return with the Father and the Spirit to dwell within believers. There will be no delay — he will not leave them "comfortless"; but he will not manifest himself to unbelievers: "the world will see me no more."

John appears to preserve a very different version of Jesus' prophetic teaching. Of course, some prophecies that the other Gospels emphasized, such as that concerning the fall of Jerusalem, had already been fulfilled by the time John wrote. Others, possibly, are stated not in their original Jewish messianic form but in terms relevant to the changed circumstances of John's time; we must examine carefully exactly what John says.

But it is evident, from comparing John with the other Gospels, that chapters 13–17 are more than simple devotional passages suitable for spiritual meditation in a relaxed hour. They contain Jesus' own final teaching on the meaning of his imminent passion and stimulating practical preparation for the coming crisis and beyond.

The Setting in Immediate Circumstances

Christ's cautious — and secret — preparations for this evening have already reminded us that this upper room discourse had its immediate context in the menacing siuation confronting Jesus and the Twelve on that fateful night. We shall miss much of Jesus' meaning if we do not appreciate the atmosphere in that guest-chamber as he spoke.

The disciples' perplexity has been described, but preparation for the future required far more than explanation. A strong emotional tension runs through the whole conversation. Fear and foreboding fed on bewilderment; the dawning realization that they were about to lose Jesus aroused suspicion that all their glowing hopes might after all be disappointed. Awareness of Jesus' peril brought dread that they themselves might share it. The upper room was shadowed with the fear of approaching tragedy, for which all except Jesus were totally unprepared.

"I go" . . . "I go" . . . "I am leaving" . . . "I was with you, but now I am going" . . . "I go away" . . . "I will no longer talk much with you" . . . "I go" . . . "I go" . . . "You will see me no more" — like *nineteen* strokes of a tolling bell Jesus reiterates the warning, together with *seven* undertones of sorrow, grief, weeping, and tribulation. Beneath all sounds *five* times the still darker note, full of regret and reproach: "betray," "betrayer," "he who eats my bread will kick back at me like a treacherous ox," "Judas went out and it was night." Nothing quite like this threnody, this long lament for Jesus, occurs anywhere else in the New Testament.

With foreboding is mingled the sharp warning of hostility. *Thirty-five* times in the five chapters John names "the world," and he uses at least sixteen pronouns referring to the world. Nothing is said here of God's loving the world, little of Christians serving the world; these references are to the world's hating (four times), the world loving its own, the world under judgment, the world not knowing the Father or Christ, the world not able to bestow peace or to receive the Spirit, and the world planning tribulation and persecution. And all the while, behind the menacing world, waiting for Jesus and then for themselves, stood "the ruler of this world."

In the opening verses of these chapters John draws the battle lines: "His hour had come to depart out of this world, . . . having loved his own who were in the world"; and at the end, "I am no more in the world, but they are in the world. . . . I pray not for the world." All is menace, hostility, and hatred out there in the darkened streets and beyond into the future: hostility that breeds fear.

No wonder, then, that "the disciples looked at one another, uncertain" and said, "What is this that he says to us? . . . We do not know what he means." No wonder, either, that Jesus spoke so much of comfort, of peace, of not letting one's heart be troubled. It was not simply lack of understanding that shook their souls with dread: "I tell you now so that when it happens you may *believe*. . . . Believe also in me." Their very faith might well be shaken.

Such was the background to that upper room conversation, to Christ's reassurances, his warnings, his call for unity, his commissioning of his men to bear fruit in such a world; the background also to his own solemnity of spirit.

> But shadow deepens now toward the close:
>   His spirit darkens with the coming doom,
> While they, in whom his heart had found repose
>   Of sympathy in good, fold close the gloom;
> For he who pours his very being forth
>   Divinely rich and pure for these, must hear
> These even now, so nigh the end, in wrath
>   Dispute pre-eminence: while, deadly near,
> Looms Peter's base denial, and each one's broken troth!
>
> (R.B.W. Noel [1834–1894],
> "And there arose a contention among them")

In such an atmosphere Jesus labored to prepare his friends, mentally and morally, for what lay ahead.

It is in the light of this setting of John 13–17 within John's Gospel, within the gospel records, and within the immediate situation that we define our approach to obviously vital chapters. Here for the last time before his death Jesus seeks to explain his mission and his destiny; to encourage and fortify his disciples against the future; to define their task and commission them for it; and so to instruct and to warn that when the storm broke over himself, and then over them, they would remember his words, understand, believe, and endure.

The seriousness and strife reflected in John 13–14 are largely alien to modern Christian faith, which expects success, blessedness, in all circumstances. In any adversity we expect instant deliverance, every prayer answered, every problem solved, every threat removed, every illness healed, every sorrow lifted, and all opposition easily overcome. Had I been present as Jesus spoke, would I have been tempted to protest, "Lord, you are getting it all wrong!"?

Meaningful
Actions

3:
An Unforgettable Gesture

JOHN 13:1-8, 12-17

Now before the feast of the Passover, when Jesus knew that his hour had come to depart out of this world to the Father, having loved his own who were in the world, he loved them to the end. And during supper, when the devil had already put it into the heart of Judas Iscariot, Simon's son, to betray him, Jesus, knowing that the Father had given all things into his hands, and that he had come from God and was going to God, rose from supper, laid aside his garments, and girded himself with a towel. Then he poured water into a basin, and began to wash the disciples' feet, and to wipe them with the towel with which he was girded. He came to Simon Peter; and Peter said to him, "Lord, do you wash my feet?" Jesus answered him, "What I am doing you do not know now, but afterward you will understand." Peter said to him, "You shall never wash my feet."

When he had washed their feet, and taken his garments, and resumed his place, he said to them, "Do you know what I have done to you? You call me Teacher and Lord; and you are right, for so I am. If I then, your Lord and Teacher, have washed your feet, you also ought to wash one another's feet. For I have given you an example, that you also should do as I have done to you. Truly, truly, I say to you, a servant is not greater than his master; nor is he who is sent greater than he who sent him. If you know these things, blessed are you if you do them.

ETCHED deeply upon every Christian imagination are certain scenes from the gospel story — Christ's baptism, the transfiguration, his entry to Jerusalem, Calvary, his meeting with Mary in the Easter garden, and many others. The list would vary from one Christian to another, but near the top of many would be the picture of Jesus girded with a towel, a bowl beside him, kneeling before one disciple after another to wash their feet.

We may guess, from the vividness and emotion with which

John writes, how deep an impression the scene left upon him; as we may divine from Peter's use, long afterwards, of an unusual phrase, "tie round yourselves the apron of humility," that another participant could never forget what Jesus did in the upper room (1 Pet. 5:5).

Nevertheless, Jesus did not set out to provide a memorable and "moving" instance of his own graciousness. Far more was at stake. If these men, the nucleus of the church that was to be, were ever to be ready for what faced them, they must be shaken to their senses. Something was deeply wrong among them. There were other matters they did not understand, in addition to the events ahead. So Jesus took action, deliberately, even sternly, and certainly effectively.

On the surface, the issue was one of simple good manners. Walking for the day about the hot, dusty streets made washing of hands and feet a necessary prelude to any meal, and a polite host would make provision for this. So Joshua, as personal servant, "poured water on the hands" of Moses; Simon the leper was rebuked for omitting the courtesy while criticizing the woman who supplied it with tears and her hair. In the hot dry season, to anoint head and feet with oil was an added luxury.

The Talmud mentions that Jewish slaves were not usually required to perform the menial task, though wives or children might do it, and a rabbi might expect it. Among an intimate group of constant companions, such as the Twelve, the youngest might assume the task, especially perhaps at Passover, when purification was essential. Then the simple act took on a religious quality. Yet neither Peter, nor John, nor Thomas, nor James "the less" would volunteer. It is clear, since Jesus "rose from the table" that supper was fully prepared; it appears that Jesus had waited for someone to offer the service — and waited in vain.

The truth is, the Twelve were scarcely in the mood for civilities, not to mention for kindness to one another. During most of that day, if not longer, there had been contention among them over "which of them was to be regarded as the greatest." Whether this rivalry had been provoked by the promise to Peter at Caesarea Philippi about the rock and the keys, or by the attempt of James and John to overreach the rest by asking prominent places in the kingdom, or by the confidence Jesus had shown in Peter and John in sending them ahead to prepare the secret rendezvous, we cannot be sure. But Luke makes it clear that the dispute continued as they gathered in the upper room (Luke 22:14, 24f.).

It would appear that Jesus first sought to win them to a better attitude by argument and appeal. Recalling with some irony how pagan rulers sought to dominate their subjects, and were rewarded by those subjects with resounding titles of "king" and "benefactor," Jesus enjoined:

> "But not so with you' . . . rather let the greatest among you become as the youngest, and the leader as one who serves. For which is the greater, one who sits at table, or one who serves? Is it not the one who sits at table? But I am among you as one who serves."

Luke does not report the effect of these words, but John at least makes clear that when the test of action came, with opportunity to show the same lowly spirit as the Master in serving each other, no one was willing. For any one to kneel before the rest to perform this humble task would be to acknowledge "inferiority" and to surrender any claim to preeminence. None would yield.

And these were the men upon whom the future depended! They seem to have learned little of the mind of Jesus. To speak lightly here of "foolish pride" is to miss the point. Socially, the Twelve were exhibiting the destructive self-assertion that attacks *every* human group and can dissolve it — the anxiety not to be put down or outdone, the determination to dominate, to be served, to rule or resign.

Individually, they were exhibiting the secret self-regard that turns the quest for righteousness into self-righteousness, that retains a hidden wish for independence and self-help even at the heart of religious faith, that turns kindness into "charity" and humility into the conscious effort to show oneself humble. Such is the constant, insidious consideration of one's own virtue that prevents our ever saying, with unselfconscious surprise, "Lord, when did we . . . ?"

In face of this stubborn incomprehension of what he would call "greatness," this refusal of his call to self-denying service, Jesus *had* to do something before that fateful night was through. What he did, the church has marveled at ever since. When no one else would make a move,

Jesus . . . rose from supper, laid aside his garments, and girded himself with a towel. Then he poured water into a basin, and began to wash the disciples' feet, and to wipe them with the towel with which he was girded . . .

not pausing at the feet of Peter, of Thomas, or of Judas.

It was a silent, yet searching, rebuke. John reveals both the real nature of their pride and the depth of their dismay as they watched with growing shame how Jesus made his meaning plain and memorable by doing for them what each in his heart had refused to do — even for him. Their recoil — "Lord, do you wash my feet? . . . You shall never wash my feet . . ." — is eloquent of their sudden self-understanding and their self-reproach.

Did they remember at that moment how, not long before, a woman had warmed his heart and won words of approval and promise by washing his feet? Peter would surely have done that for Jesus — and lived thereafter in the glow of a memorable act of devotion! To sit passively accepting such service from Christ implied that he — Peter! — *needed* washing; implied that so far from being leader in the kingdom community, he was still a suppliant in need of gracious help, having still to cry "Depart from me, for I am a sinful man, O Lord. . . ."

If Christ's initiative was a rebuke, his insistence sharpened it. They *must* accept his ministry — or have no part with him. He did not come to be served, but to serve, and they needed his service. They must be cleansed — not least, of this self-sufficient, self-isolating pride. Each had better realize at once that the servant is never greater than his master (v. 16).

Taking his place again at the table, Jesus unfolded the full meaning of his acted reproach: "Do you know what I have done to you?"

First, there were the titles they readily used for him. "You call me Teacher and Lord; and you are right, for so I am." Why, then, do his words mean so little to them, does his spirit so rarely kindle theirs, or do his own actions fail to evoke similar actions from them? No language is quite so trite, so empty, as devotional talk without active meaning, religious profession without corresponding performance. "Why do you call me 'Lord, Lord' and not do what I tell you?" Jesus had asked earlier, adding, "Not every one who says to me 'Lord, Lord' shall enter the kingdom of heaven but he who *doeth* . . ." (Luke 6:46; Matt.

21

7:21). And so here he repeats, "If you know these things, happy are you if you do them." Jesus had no use at all for idle compliments.

Next, Jesus turned to their relation with each other. So much would depend in the future upon that, and he returns to it again and again. Though their Lord and Master, he had washed their feet — and so they should wash, not *his* but *one another's*. He would not accept for himself a ministry that they refused toward each other.

The pride that divided them must go. They must serve each other and learn to accept service from each other. They must not think that they can serve him *instead*. John does not record the verdict passed in the parable of judgment, "Inasmuch as you did it not to one of the least of these, you did it not to me," but the principle is implied here, and perhaps also in verse 20, which otherwise seems out of place: "he who receives any one whom I send receives me. . . ." As men and women treat those who are his, so they are treating him: disciples who will not wash each other's feet need not think to wash their Lord's.

Everyone wishes to add "of course, we need not take this literally" and to translate the essential meaning into more innocuous forms of social service, caring situations, even bishops' aprons! We must be careful of our motives here. For many years in the apostolic church, "washing the feet of the saints" remained a "good deed" testifying to Christian character (1 Tim. 5:10), and some groups of believers still practice this rite. Others have stooped to commensurable tasks, serving the leprous, the vicious, and the depraved, extending the literal meaning in unmeasured faithfulness. It is certain that we shall never "wash one another's feet" in ways socially acceptable and personally comfortable if we are determined that in no circumstances would we ever do it literally.

Finally, Jesus makes that single action, at that crucial moment, a standard for discipleship henceforward: "I have given you an example, that you also should do as I have done to you." So at once we confront the central motif of Christian ethics, the imitation of Christ.

That motif has assumed many forms in the long adventure of Christian discipleship, from an outward copying of the celibate, itinerant pattern of Christ's earthly life by the medieval monk to the mystic inner dialogue with Christ of Thomas a Kempis; from the "assimilation to God" of the early Fathers to "following in his steps," the motto of the modern Christian activist, or "being formed with the form of Christ" with Dietrich Bonhoeffer. In all versions of the "imitation" ideal, Christ remains sole pattern and exemplar of his own teaching, the goal of hearts devoted to him, the incarnation of all that the Christian longs to be.

"Imitation of Christ," "being conformed to the image of God's Son," "being changed into the same image as by the Spirit," "pure as he is pure," "like him, because we shall see him as he is" — the idea is everywhere in the New Testament. Here in the upper room it is presented to us, as it was to the Twelve, in all its clarity and depth. For in the special example of lowly self-denying service of others, even the least attractive and deserving, the Christ-ideal challenges head-on the essential selfishness of unaided human nature. At the same time, the motive of our imitation is defined with clear emphasis — "If I . . . have washed your feet, you also ought to wash one another's feet. . . . You also should do as I have done to you. . . ." And again a little later, "as I have loved you, that you also love one another."

We are not called to watch how Jesus behaves toward others, and then admiringly set ourselves to copy him. That ministers to self-righteousness. We are called to accept his washing of our feet, to let him minister to our deep need, to find our own hope and comfort in his love — and then, in adoring *gratitude* to treat others as our Lord has treated us.

It was a truly unforgettable gesture. "Love for Christ himself, expressed in genuine likeness to him, especially in his attitude towards the least and neediest of men, and all because of what we ourselves have received from him": that firm definition of discipleship is focused sharply before these quarreling men at the outset of that last decisive evening. None could misunderstand; one refused the challenge. Every Christian now knows that following Christ will bring him, some time, somewhere, somehow, to kneel beside Jesus with a towel in his hands.

All that is clear if we look only at the surface of the story. But there is much more.

THE NIGHT HE WAS BETRAYED

To the editor: "I was was walking along Gordon Street at about 9.40 a.m. and on looking towards Central Station I saw something which I feel is worthy of note. One of our less fortunate citizens who had been sleeping in one of the grids outside the station sat up, and just then a woman approached him, laid her bag and umbrella down, and proceeded to put on his boots, which he had obviously removed for comfort. I felt greatly heartened. . . ."

(Letter to *Glasgow Evening Times*, Christmas 1977)

4:
—And So Much More

JOHN 12:36-41; 13:1-10

When Jesus had said this, he departed and hid himself from them. Though he had done so many signs before them, yet they did not believe in him; it was that the word spoken by the prophet Isaiah might be fulfilled:

"Lord, who has believed our report,
and to whom has the arm of the Lord been revealed?"

Therefore they could not believe. For Isaiah again said,

"He has blinded their eyes and hardened their heart,
lest they should see with their eyes and perceive with their
*   heart,*
and turn for me to heal them."

Isaiah said this because he saw his glory and spoke of him.
*   Now before the feast of the Passover, when Jesus knew that his hour had come to depart out of this world to the Father, having loved his own who were in the world, he loved them to the end. And during supper, when the devil had already put it into the heart of Judas Iscariot, Simon's son, to betray him, Jesus, knowing that the Father had given all things into his hands, and that he had come from God and was going to God, rose from supper, laid aside his garments, and girded himself with a towel. Then he poured water into a basin, and began to wash the disciples' feet, and to wipe them with the towel with which he was girded. He came to Simon Peter; and Peter said to him, "Lord, do you wash my feet?" Jesus answered him, "What I am doing you do not know now, but afterward you will understand." Peter said to him, "You shall never wash my feet." Jesus answered him, "If I do not wash you, you have no part in me." Simon Peter said to him, "Lord, not my feet only but also my hands and my head!" Jesus said to him, "He who has bathed does not need to wash, except for his feet, but he is clean all over; and you are clean, but not all of you."*

25

JOHN has thought long and deeply about the stories he recalls. The straightforward account of the healing of a blind man in Jerusalem becomes, in John's reflection, both an illustration of Christ's claim to be the light of the world and a provocation for an argument with Pharisees about whether, in quite another sense, they "see" or "do not see" (9:5, 39f.).

When John has finished telling of the feeding of five thousand from a boy's lunch, layer upon layer of meaning may be discerned within the story. Beside the miracle picnic on the hillside, there is the overtone of Passover (6:4) lending a formal religious flavor to the meal. This is recognized as a "sign," and the people acclaim Jesus as "the" prophet, foretold by Moses (v. 14). An attempt is made to crown Jesus by force, which brings a messianic "coronation-feast" interpretation to the open-air repast (v. 15).

The next day, in the synagogue at Capernaum, Jesus himself takes the bread for text to speak of the food that endures to eternal life (v. 27). This again provokes comparison with Moses, who also provided "heavenly bread," though the Jewish fathers did not live forever. To this, Jesus replies that he is the true bread from heaven (vv. 33–35). This arouses protest, for the hearers claim to know Jesus' earthly parentage (v. 42), to which Jesus answers by reasserting that he came from heaven in order that those who "eat of this bread" may live forever (v. 51). When this language again evokes protest, Jesus sharpens it to "eat the flesh of the son of man and drink his blood . . ." (v. 53) — and we are beside the Lord's table. Nevertheless, this again, in the end, depends upon believing the words that convey spirit and life (vv. 63f.).

However cautious and even skeptical we may rightly be about claims to discover "deeper meanings" within Scripture, it can hardly be denied that here are seven or eight connected meanings that one by one develop the significance of that marvelous original story of the hungry crowd fed in the evening sunshine.

That certainly does not justify *inventing* as many meanings as ingenuity can suggest: it does mean that we should watch for the hints *that John himself provides* to warn us that something more is implied than appears on the surface. In his story of the washing of the disciples' feet, such hints are plentiful.

26

Clues to Deeper Meaning

1. Both the setting of chapters 13–17 within John's Gospel and comparison with the other Gospels suggest that the whole section is John's introduction to the story of Christ's passion; yet that must raise the question of whether the opening incident — the feet-washing — is relevant, or quite irrelevant, to that passion preparation. We cannot forget that this was the night on which Jesus was betrayed, arrested, and tried, or that the talk was full of his "going away." John's introduction to all this is not by talk of "ransom," or by describing the Lord's supper, but by the "unforgettable gesture" of washing the disciples' feet. Is John hinting that as Jesus turns from the crowd toward his cross, his first action throws light upon his purpose?

2. We might not think so, but for that magnificent preamble:

> Now before the feast of the Passover, when Jesus knew that his hour had come to depart out of this world to the Father, having loved his own who were in the world, he loved them to the end. And during supper, when the devil had already put it into the heart of Judas Iscariot, Simon's son, to betray him, Jesus, knowing that the Father had given all things into his hands, and that he had come from God and was going to God, rose from supper. . . .

That would seem a crashing anticlimax, if the words were not so familiar.

Here is a deliberate setting of the story against the background of the Passover. Here is a solemn reminder that the awaited hour has struck for Jesus, with repeated references to his departure. The divine love that underlay Christ's whole mission is brought to mind as enduring to the "end." The demonic forces working in the background are explicitly mentioned, along with the firmer resolution of Judas to betray Jesus. Christ's sovereignty — "all things in his hands" — and that unique, breathtaking destiny that brought him out of eternity through this world to return to God again are recalled — all to introduce the simple statement that Jesus rose from the table?

That can scarcely be true. Such weight of theological, moral, historical, and demonic allusion clearly compels us to expect not *merely* a kind deed and a lesson in Christian manners, but some massive divine self-disclosure. There must be more within this story than at first appears, to justify that introduction; something tremendous is afoot, connected with his coming "departure."

3. It is, however, the explicit words of Jesus that warn us most powerfully to consider what we are reading. "Do you know what I have done to you?" he asks, as if there could be anything incomprehensible about water and a bowl, washing and a towel. "What I am doing you do not know now, but afterward you will understand" (v. 7). What can that possibly mean? Upon what future event does their understanding of *clean feet* depend — and what is there to understand, that Peter cannot see at once?

Again, "If I do not wash you, you have no part in me" (v. 8). There is something about this act absolutely essential to any relationship with Christ! Nothing else in the whole New Testament would support the idea that literal feet-washing, whether by Jesus or by one's fellow disciples, is essential to salvation, and such a condition of relationship is never imposed upon others. Something much more important than clean feet is plainly in Christ's thought.

Once more: Jesus said, "He who has bathed does not need to wash, except for his feet, but he is clean all over; and you are clean, but not all of you." John adds the explanation: "For he knew who was to betray him; that was why he said 'You are not all clean.'" The precise application of these words admittedly is obscure, but it can scarcely be doubted that they refer to a cleansing other than that of the bowl and towel, which in fact Judas *had* received.

With all due caution, we are pressed by these mysterious words of Jesus, even more than by John's arrangement of the story and his sonerous preamble, to accept that some abiding, essential, and saving significance is being "read into" the simple act of washing a friend's feet. We have here more than a lesson in Christian behavior, far-searching though that was.

"As One Who Serves"

From the whole pattern of John's Gospel we were led to expect that everything said and done in the upper room would contribute to Christ's further self-manifestation to his disciples, with a view to their enduring faith when the world's storm broke. Constantly (we said) Jesus, in John, seeks to illumine who he is and what is his mission from the Father. The question is, therefore, what "deeper meaning" does the story of the feet-washing reveal concerning the person and work of Jesus?

At once there springs to mind John's intense concentration, in this passage, upon the figure of Jesus. His is the initiative in the opening scene, as he is the speaker throughout most of the subsequent dialogue. In the opening words, Jesus' knowledge, his "hour," his love, his betrayal, his having all things, and his coming from God and going to God set the stage. During the action, Peter protests — not at having his feet washed at all, but at who is doing it. As Jesus resumes his seat, it is with the titles they commonly use for himself that he begins the explanation; while it is to his own spirit and attitude that he directs them for an example.

If John's concentration upon Jesus is not in doubt, neither is the character in which Jesus is here represented. Clearly, un-ambiguously, he is "one who serves." If the towel and basin did not proclaim it, his own words would do so: "If I . . . have washed your feet, you also ought to wash one another's feet . . . . a *servant* is not greater than his master. . . ." The theme of the final self-manifestation of Jesus to his men is *the Servant* of God and of men.

The words "a servant is not greater than his master" occur in Matthew and Luke in a different setting; their echo here makes a fitting caption to the scene just witnessed. Jesus has acted the part of the Servant before adding that title to those of Teacher and Lord, which he says are rightly his — "for so I am."

The identification of Jesus with the Servant of God and man is so important to the whole passage that we must take the greatest care to ensure that we are not misinterpreting John. That Jesus is "Servant of the Lord" at his baptism, speaks of himself so (Luke 22:27), and is so described in Matthew 12:17ff.; Acts 3:25; 4:27, 30; 8:30f.; Philippians 2:5ff.; and 1 Peter 2:22f. does not prove that John has the Servant prophecies in mind in 13:1f., though we must remember how familiar this identifica-tion was by the time John wrote.

More to the point is that quarrel among the Twelve over who should have precedence. In Mark, Jesus comments upon that contention by declaring that greatness lies in service, as he him-self had come "not to be served but to serve, and to give his life a ransom for many" — a clear echo of Isaiah's Song of the Suffering Servant (52:13–53:12). At precisely that point John shows Jesus acting the part of the Servant to his disciples.

John leaves us in no doubt that this is his meaning by himself quoting the same Servant prophecy in his lead-in to the story. As Jesus closes his public ministry (chap. 12), John comments upon the nation's rejection of him in words the prophet had used to comment on the rejection of the Servant of the Lord (12:38f.), adding that "Isaiah spoke of [Jesus]." Then John tells of Jesus the Servant washing the disciples' feet.

At the end of the evening, Jesus went forth to his arrest and trial, during which (in John's account) much is made of his innocence and his silence. Afterward, with the help of Nicodemus, his body was laid in the tomb of Joseph of Arimathea. As Isaiah's Servant prophecy had foretold, he was like a lamb dumb before its shearers; he had done no violence; he was numbered with the transgressors; and yet he was with the rich in his death. In telling the passion story, John has the Servant prophecies clearly in mind.

The conclusion is inescapable. As with the miracle of the feeding of the five thousand (and with much else in his Gospel), so with the feet-washing: John chooses a straightforward, though sufficiently wonderful, incident in Christ's ministry to convey the most profound evangelical truth. He is saying that, in the first action of Jesus in the upper room, the fitting category was chosen in which Christ's final self-manifestation should be expressed, the category of the Servant. As in the prophecies upon this theme, the service of the Servant is offered first to God, and secondarily to men; and it culminates in the suffering of rejection and death.

That is John's clue, and Christ's own explanation of the meaning of his imminent passion. He will suffer as the Servant of God and men. John 13 takes its place with the other great passages in the New Testament that dwell upon the work of Jesus as Servant of the Lord.

John 13 thus offers some explanation, otherwise not easy to find, of how the Servant motif came to possess so early, so widespread, and so central a place in Christian thought. Without it, Mark 10:45 stands almost alone, until Matthew's Gospel was written later on. John's story would surely write it upon the church's mind.

At first sight it might seem surprising that John should introduce so late in his Gospel an idea, and title, so vital and far-reaching for our understanding of Jesus. But glancing back through the Gospel, we realize that all John's emphasis concerning Jesus, at least from chapter 5, has been upon his subordination, dependence, and obedience. "The Son can do nothing of his own accord, but only what he sees the Father doing. . . . as the Father raises the dead, . . . so also the Son. . . . the Father . . . has *given* all judgment to the Son. . . . has *granted* the Son to have life in himself, and has *given* him authority. . . . I can do nothing on my own authority; as I hear, I judge . . . I seek not my own will but the will of him who sent me. . . . the works which the Father has given me to accomplish. . . . My teaching is not mine but his who sent me. . . . I have not come of my own accord. . . . I do nothing on my own authority but speak as the Father taught me. . . . I came to do the will of him who sent me. . . . I do always what pleases him. . . . My refreshment is to do the will of him who sent me. . . . As the Father has given me commandment, so I do. . . ."

This astonishing list of disclaimers and protestations is from first to last the language of the Servant of God, who has no initiative, no authority, no word or deeds of his own, but is wholly subservient, obedient, and dependent toward the one who sent him. And as he comes, speaks, and acts at the Father's will, so he will die "as the Father has commanded." "For this reason the Father loves me, because I lay down my life. . . . No one takes it from me, but I lay it down of my own accord" (there lies the willing Servant's freedom); "I have power to lay it down and I have power to take it again; this charge I have received from my Father" (there lies the Servant's obedience).

Thus, throughout John's Gospel, the Servant is revealed as the unresisting, transparent vehicle of the divine will, the perfect, undistorting mirror of the Father whom "no man has seen or can see" — except in Christ.

The story of the washing of the disciples' feet turns out to be the final, and superb, expression of John's main thesis concerning the person of Jesus: from first to last, he is the obedient and dependent Servant of God and men. Nothing is more distinctive, or more central, in Christianity than the realization that man needs someone to do for him what desperately needs to be done, but which he cannot possibly do for himself. That is the task of the Servant.

So the central motif of Christian ethics and the central theme of Christian theology shine together in the kneeling figure with the basin and towel. By it we are challenged, first to let him serve us in our utmost need, then to go forth imitating his spirit, as servants of the Servant of the Lord.

> *O lowly majesty,*
>   *Lofty in lowliness,*
> *Blest Saviour, who am I*
>   *To share thy blessedness?*
> *Yet thou hast called me, even me,*
> *Servant divine, to follow thee.*
> (G.W. Briggs [1875–1959], "Son of the Lord Most High")

Strange that among all the titles Christians use for Jesus in hymns, prayers, worship, and conversation the rarest of all is "Servant of the Lord." Or is it strange?

5:
The Servant's Task

JOHN 13:8b–11; 17:17–19

Jesus answered him, "If I do not wash you, you have no part in me." Simon Peter said to him, "Lord, not my feet only but also my hands and my head!" Jesus said to him, "He who has bathed does not need to wash, except for his feet, but he is clean all over; and you are clean, but not all of you." For he knew who was to betray him; that was why he said, "You are not all clean."

"Sanctify them in the truth; thy word is truth. As thou didst send me into the world, so I have sent them into the world. And for their sake I consecrate myself, that they also may be consecrated in truth."

T HERE is no point in simply *being* a servant, unless to accomplish some specific task. What is the work that only the appointed Servant of the Lord can do?

Isaiah spoke of the Servant's establishing justice in the earth, without strife or clamor. He is to bring Jacob back to God, to restore Israel, and to offer salvation to the ends of the earth. To accomplish this, the Servant will bear our griefs and carry our sorrows. God will lay on him our iniquities, and he will, though innocent, be numbered with transgressors and make intercession for sinners. Matthew echoes part of Isaiah's thought (Matt. 12:17f.).

Paul thinks, rather, of the example of humility set for Christian minds by Christ's voluntary choice of the servant role (Phil. 2). Writing to Christian servants, Peter recalls the divine Servant's meekness under affliction, and his healing death (1 Pet. 2:20ff.). John would certainly include in the work the Servant is sent to do, revealing the unseen Father, speaking God's word, and doing God's will. Yet these thoughts are not present in John 13:1–20 to explain the Servant's service; nor do these tasks explain Christ's imminent passion. Why must the Servant die? We must again examine carefully what John actually says.

1. The immediate picture of the Servant in John 13 leaves no doubt that his task has something to do with cleansing. Water, a basin, a towel, washed feet, "wash" (eight times), and the whole story focus plainly upon an act of purification. Jesus is seen here not healing, preaching, bearing infirmities, establishing justice, or carrying sins, but washing feet. Only willfulness could miss the implication that the Servant is sent to cleanse the soiled feet of humankind.

2. Christ's own interpretation of his action is in the same terms: "you are clean," "bathed," "clean all over," "clean." Peter's reaction to the warning "If I do not wash you, you have no part in me" likewise implies that cleansing is the theme — "Lord, not my feet only but also my hands and my head." Peter is thinking of the insistence of rabbis upon *complete* purification in all ritual washings, as in proselyte baptism.

Later that evening Jesus spoke of pruning the vine of God, using again the same word "cleanse," and repeating "you are clean." Later still he prayed that the disciples might be "sanctified," "kept from evil." For whatever reason, the thought of purification loomed large in Christ's mind on that evening of crowded thought.

3. This should not surprise us. For John has already said that the Passover was at hand and many went up to Jerusalem to purify themselves (11:55); innumerable immersion pools existed for this purpose in the city's vicinity. The Passover is recalled again in 13:1. No Jew would celebrate this festival of double liberation, from Egypt and from Exile, a festival now possessing overtones of messianic hope, without most scrupulous purification.

Jesus once rebuked the scribes and Pharisees for being like tombs that were beautiful on the outside but unclean within, thus recalling the zeal with which, at this season, graves were freshly marked and tombs whitewashed, lest any pilgrim be accidentally defiled. Paul, too, recalls the "fit of spring-cleaning" with which the whole nation was seized, houses, cupboards, cities, and countryside all being cleansed —

> Christ, our paschal lamb, has been sacrificed. Let us, therefore, celebrate the festival, not with the old leaven, the leaven of malice and evil, but with the unleavened bread of sincerity and truth.

So readily, to a Jewish mind, did Passover suggest the need for self-cleansing.

At Jesus' trial the next morning, the priests refused to enter Pilate's court lest they be defiled — accidental contact with things "gentile" being more feared than the murderous thoughts that brought them there! Admittedly, this timing creates some uncertainty whether the meal in the upper room could have been Passover; but no devout Jew would partake of *any* sacred meal at that time without due attention to the purification rites. A general purification earlier in the day still left need that "he who has bathed" should after walking wash his feet (v. 10). The refusal of any among the Twelve to perform this service was more than a breach of good manners; it was a triumph of pride over piety.

John's repeated reference to the Passover is thus no mere date, but a major clue to his meaning. Jesus is moving forward to the Passover that was to cost him his life, in fulfillment of the divine mission entrusted to him, later defined in the words "to purify for himself a people of his own" (Titus 2:14). When the Servant of the Lord kneels before men with basin and towel, he is seen at his essential task.

This conception of Christ's work is to modern Christians both unfamiliar and unwelcome. This is partly because the sense of the holiness of God has died out of modern religion, and partly because the age-old ritual that expressed it is unknown to us. Sacrificial worship and simple public prayer demanded of Israel "clean hands," "bodies washed with pure water," garments newly laundered. Such ritual rules were no play-acting; they enshrined the spiritual command "Be ye holy, for I am holy, says the Lord."

The prophets knew well that ritual cleanness was not enough, but in demanding more rigorous cleansing they still used the ritual language:

> I will sprinkle clean water upon you, and you shall be clean from all your uncleannesses, and from all your idols I will cleanse you. A new heart will I give you . . . on the day that I cleanse you from all your iniquities. . . . On that day there shall be a fountain opened for the house of David . . . to cleanse them from sin and uncleanness.

So Ezekiel and Zechariah; more vividly, this need was held before the people in the practice of proselyte baptism, by which "unclean" gentiles were purified for admission to the people of God. The Baptist pressed home the same truth relentlessly, demanding in preparation for the coming of Messiah a baptism of repentance, even from Jews. The apostles retained the same thought in phrases like "Rise and be baptised, and *wash away* your sins . . ."; "You were *washed* . . . in the name of the Lord Jesus"; "the *washing* of regeneration."

The Greeks had a myth of the mighty Hercules, commissioned by the gods to undertake immense tasks. Among them was the cleansing of the famous Augean stables, where generations of great horses had been bred, of the accumulated filth of many years. He accomplished the task by diverting a mighty river through the stalls. So in its own way, the Greek mind confirms the Jews' insight that the world needs, among many other things, a radical, profound, and permanent *purification*. Modern psychology uses other terms, but testifies often to the same deep need of mental purgation.

The form, the commentary, and the timing of the feet-washing story show that to John's way of thinking, Jesus, as Servant of the Lord, also accepted the divine mission to cleanse the defiled minds and hearts of men and women — though not by strength, or miracle, but by suffering. For the feet-washing was not only Jesus' response to the need for Passover purification; it was also the prelude to his passion.

What is this Cleansing?

One main purpose of the upper room interview was to prepare the disciples for Calvary; for the future's sake, they must understand why Jesus must *die*. John has provided already numerous hints and illustrations of the meaning of Christ's death —

> Jesus died as the lamb of God, taking away the sin of the world;
> Jesus died as a serpent on a pole, to whom to look brought healing and life;
> Jesus died as the bread of life, broken to nourish humankind;
> Jesus died as the good shepherd defending his sheep;
> Jesus died as a grain of wheat that falls into soil, that it might grow;

Jesus died as setting up a magnetic pylon, drawing all
    hearts unto him;
Jesus died as judging and breaking the power of evil
    (12:31);
Jesus died as victor over the prince of this world

— but (unless "lamb of God" originally implied "Servant of the
Lord," as is possible) John 13 is the only passage where John
represents the coming cross as the culmination of the Servant's
task, to wash the feet of humankind.

The Baptist's words on the opening pages of the Gospel
prove to be central to the author's understanding of its close. We
are indeed to behold the lamb — and Servant — taking away the
accumulated sin of the world. An obscure, but intriguing, comment in John's account of Christ's death confirms this view:

> One of the soldiers pierced his side with a spear, and at once
> there came out blood and water. He who saw it has borne
> witness — his testimony is true, and he knows that he tells
> the truth — that you also may believe.

Believe what? Something important, obviously, from the underlined testimony. Amid the obscurity this surely is clear: John
would have us believe that from the wounded heart of the dying
Savior flowed the cleansing stream that would wash away the
defilement of the world. John would have his readers pray:

> Let the water and the blood
> From thy riven side which flowed
> Be of sin the double cure:
> Cleanse me from its guilt, and power.
> > (A.M. Toplady [1740–1778], "Rock of Ages")

We may be surprised to find water and blood together referred to in this way as means of purification. Later, Jesus will
say, "You are already made clean *by the word* which I have
spoken to you."

1. Cleansing by the *word* is closely echoed in the prayer of
Jesus for the Eleven: "Sanctify them in the truth: thy word is
truth." The meaning lies, in all probability, in John's profound
conception of truth as not only that which illumines the mind
but also something to be expressed practically in behavior ("*doing*
the truth"), and to be incarnated in personality itself ("the truth

in you"). (The "cleansing by *pruning*," to which also Jesus refers, is probably best understood in the light of Jesus' next action, still to be considered.)

2. The Jewish rituals, and a prophetic interpretation of them, prepare us to understand cleansing by *water,* but its Christian significance is harder to interpret with confidence. When Jesus warned Nicodemus that he needed to be born of water and of the Spirit, he appears to be saying that John's baptism of repentance and something *more* were necessary to enter the kingdom. Less positively, the story of the blind man who washed and "came seeing" seems to hint at illumination through baptism — as an early church writer (Justin) understood it. The later phrases "be baptized, washing . . . ," "you were washed . . . in the name of the Lord Jesus," and "washing of regeneration" (as we have seen) also link baptism with cleansing by water.

To many, such an interpretation seems to press the allusion to water much too hard. The difficulty is to find anything else in apostolic Christian experience to which words like "If I do not wash you, you have no part with me," spoken with basin, water, and towel at hand, could plausibly be referred. Is not John saying, following Jesus (and as Paul would say), that unless disciples are "baptized into Christ's death," they have no part in him?

There is no question that in the church for which John wrote, baptism was universally observed as initiation into Christian life, or that John's record would be read with this in mind. We know too that the early church was for long exercised about sins following baptism — was further "cleansing" possible? There are textual difficulties about the precise wording of Jesus' reply to Peter, "He who has bathed does not need to wash [except for his feet(?)] but he is clean all over. . . ." If that version is correct, it may be that John is recalling words that exclude the dangerous idea that one good wash suffices for life. For however earnestly we enter the Christian life, we do fall into sin as we go on, and we do need the perpetual purification that Jesus taught us to pray for.

We have reasons, therefore, for saying that to link cleansing by water with Christian baptism is at any rate not *wrong*.

3. Yet cleansing by the word and cleansing by the water do not clearly necessitate the death of the Servant. The cleansing of the mind by truth and of the outward life by public baptism

(if that is the meaning here) rest upon a much more radical and costly cleansing of sinful men by the sacrifice of the Servant. Water and *blood* flowed from the side of Christ: it was as an offered lamb that he was to take away the sin of the world. The prophet whom John has just quoted (12:38ff.) had declared that the Servant would be despised and rejected, wounded for our transgressions, oppressed, afflicted, and cut off out of the land of the living, because he bore the sin of many.

It is true that the idea of washing in blood occurs in the New Testament only at Revelation 7:14 (and then by means of a Greek word different from that in John 13); true, too, that such a thought would be as repugnant to Jewish minds as to ours. But the general idea of purification by sacrifice, alongside that of purification by water, was an essential part of Hebrew religion and of early Christian thought. A Christian Jew could declare that "under the law almost everything is purified with blood," while the First Epistle of John, promising cleansing from all unrighteousness, can add "the blood of Jesus . . . cleanses us from all sin."

If, then, John means that the essential work of the Servant for God and men is to cleanse away sin through his passion, the purifying, expiatory power of sacrifice for sin is the metaphor being used. Neither the meaning nor the metaphor can be left behind if the work of Christ the Servant is to be fully understood in modern Christianity. The cleansing virtue of his purifying death is "applied," so to speak, to each believing soul through the public commitment that each convert makes in baptism to die and rise with him to new life. And that act of baptism is itself the acceptance of the saving word of Christ that purifies mind, imagination, and conscience. Thousands have testified that the word of the cross, accepted and shared in baptism, does save and cleanse the sinful life.

No debate is possible as to the relevance of such language to contemporary society. The defiling influences in modern life are too obvious, whether we prefer to emphasize their social aspect (as vice, environment, heredity, corruption), or their psychological depth (as obsessive guilt, addiction, self-negation, "inadequacy," or moral sickness), or their religious dimension (as disobedience and sin). As usual, Shakespeare expresses powerfully the human experience:

> Canst thou not minister to a mind diseased,
> Pluck from the memory a rooted sorrow,
> Raze out the written troubles of the brain,
> And with some sweet oblivious antidote
> Cleanse the stuff'd bosom of that perilous stuff
> Which weighs upon the heart?

To which Shakespeare's doctor replies,

> Therein the patient
> Must minister to himself. . . .
>
> (*Macbeth*, V. iii. 40-46)

But the defiled can do little to cleanse themselves. Personal penitence must be somewhere involved:

> Drop, drop slow tears
> And bathe those beauteous feet
> Which brought from heaven
> The news and Prince of peace:
> Cease not, wet eyes,
> His mercies to entreat;
> To cry for vengeance
> Sin doth never cease.
> In your deep floods
> Drown all my faults and fears:
> Nor let his eye
> See sin, but through my tears.
>
> (Phinehas Fletcher [1582–1650], "Drop, drop slow tears")

Penitence is necessary, but it is equally true that

> Could my zeal no respite know,
> Could my tears for ever flow,
> All for sin could not atone;
> *Thou must save, and thou alone.*
>
> (A.M. Toplady [1740–1778], "Rock of Ages")

That, too, must be remembered. Like Peter, if we are not cleansed by the gentle Servant of God, we have no part in him.

But what, precisely, does this mean? We are ever in danger of losing the truth within familiar — or unfamiliar — metaphors. It *means* what Christianity has ever made central to the gospel: that for every stained, defiled, corrupted soul of man or woman there is forgiveness with God; forgiveness made available, made possible, made morally defensible by expiation, by Christ's purifying, sin-removing acceptance of others' responsibility, for love's pure sake. In that forgiving, expiating love lies hope for the helpless, the soiled, the alienated, and the disturbed. For in the purifying power of a true religious experience lies personal renewal, reorientation, and regeneration.

Few passages, even of Scripture, are so loaded with meaning as John 13. The "unforgettable gesture" that rebuked rivalry, set an example of divine humility, and illustrated the duty of serving one another, when seen against its total context, turns out to be also a condensed theological statement. It enshrines the supreme self-disclosure of Jesus as Servant of the Lord, commissioned to suffer in order to purify humankind. From the figure of the kneeling Jesus with water and a towel, the line runs swift and straight to the riven side whence flows the tide that washes clean the sin of all humanity.

Create in me a clean heart, O God, and renew a right spirit within me.

> *Wash me, and make me thus Thine own,*
> *Wash me —and mine Thou art:*
> *Wash me, but not my feet alone,*
> *My hands, my head, my heart!*
(Charles Wesley [1707–1778], "Forever here my rest shall be")

6:
The Expulsion of Judas

JOHN 13:11, 18–35

For he knew who was to betray him; that was why he said, "You are not all clean."

"I am not speaking of you all; I know whom I have chosen; it is that the scripture may be fulfilled, 'He who ate my bread has lifted his heel against me.' I tell you this now, before it takes place, that when it does take place you may believe that I am he. Truly, truly, I say to you, he who receives any one whom I send receives me; and he who receives me receives him who sent me."

When Jesus had thus spoken, he was troubled in spirit, and testified, "Truly, truly, I say to you, one of you will betray me." The disciples looked at one another, uncertain of whom he spoke. One of his disciples, whom Jesus loved, was lying close to the breast of Jesus; so Simon Peter beckoned to him and said, "Tell us who it is of whom he speaks." So lying thus, close to the breast of Jesus, he said to him, "Lord, who is it?" Jesus answered, "It is he to whom I shall give this morsel when I have dipped it." So when he had dipped the morsel, he gave it to Judas, the son of Simon Iscariot. Then after the morsel, Satan entered into him. Jesus said to him, "What you are going to do, do quickly." Now no one at the table knew why he said this to him. Some thought that, because Judas had the money box, Jesus was telling him, "Buy what we need for the feast"; or, that he should give something to the poor. So, after receiving the morsel, he immediately went out; and it was night.

When he had gone out, Jesus said, "Now is the Son of man glorified, and in him God is glorified; if God is glorified in him, God will also glorify him in himself, and glorify him at once. Little children, yet a little while I am with you. You will seek me; and as I said to the Jews so now I say to you, 'Where I am going you cannot come.' A new commandment I give to you, that you love one another; even as I have loved you, that you also love one another. By this all men will know that you are my disciples, if you have love for one another."

To have your feet washed, even by Jesus himself, is no guarantee that you are clean. Purification must reach inward, and also outward — the group must be cleansed. "You are clean," said Jesus, "but not all of you"; and John explains, "he knew who was to betray him; that was why he said, 'you are not all clean.'"

As Jesus proceeded to his second deliberate action in that darkening upper room, his brow clouded, his eyes grew troubled (v. 21), and his voice became sombre, as the questions that followed show. John has mentioned the demonic influence that took shape in the heart of Judas: now Jesus deals firmly with that hidden menace, with an unanswerable authority that is almost frightening. "I am not speaking of you all; . . . one of you will betray me."

One purpose in the Master's mind was to prepare the disciples for the real shock that one of them would play the treacherous part in the coming catastrophe. His own sense of horror at such betrayal prompts the expressions "he who ate my bread," breaking the sacred covenant of hospitality, "has lifted his heel against me," like a treacherous, rebellious beast that lashes out at its master; so wild and blind will be the action of one professing discipleship.

"I tell you this now, before it takes place, that when it does take place you may believe that I am he." To be forewarned is to be fortified against dismay. Jesus is not taken by surprise. "I know whom I have chosen" — their potential, their character, their struggles — and the one who has turned against me. Nor is the coming crime unforeseen in the long purposes of God. It happens "that the scripture may be fulfilled." The disciple may find reassurance and the scoffer will be robbed of a weapon of scorn in the fact that all is happening within divine control. Christ's own careful preparation for this evening confirms that all was known to him beforehand.

The Master's other purpose was to cleanse the disciple-band, the nucleus of the new people for God. Frequently in Old Testament days, the whole people of Israel were called to purify themselves for some great occasion of revelation or of festival. Here in Jesus' words the same corporate dimension of Passover purification is expressed: "you are clean, but not all of you." Later, the same thought of group cleansing will underlie his words about the pruning ("cleansing") of the vine that God has newly planted in the earth. As God cannot use (though he may overrule) the unclean soul, so he cannot use (though he may override) the unclean community, nation, remnant, church. When appeal fails, he will cleanse by judgment.

The moment has arrived for such final appeal — or judgment. This is Christ's second deliberate action on that decisive evening. Within the nucleus of the coming church lies an element of uncleanness, resistance, and treachery that must be removed. The rest of the Twelve were far from perfect; they were unprepared and disunited, but they were malleable. One was becoming obdurate. Fear, foreboding, and rivalry undermine, but they do not defile: the intention to betray was of another kind, and had to be purged. Judas must be brought to self-understanding, if necessary to self-exclusion.

The Enigma of Judas

John is sure that Jesus knew what was in man (2:25). The call of Judas into discipleship could not have been error, or accident. John insists also upon Jesus' truth and integrity: the call of Judas could not have been pretence, or a trap to lure him to disaster. Judas was "chosen" (6:70) because he had qualities that could have made a worthy disciple, and he was given his privileged opportunity, as were the others. To question this would be to impugn Jesus' honesty toward him.

Judas' bitter remorse and his despairing attempt to stay the harm he had done (ending, according to one account, in suicide; (Matt. 27:3ff.; see Acts 1:18f.) reveal a remnant of conscience at work. Matthew's remark that this was "when Judas saw that Jesus was condemned" makes us wonder if Judas had not expected the matter to go so far, or even had some thought of forcing Jesus to show his hand in power.

On the other side, Judas like the rest had weaknesses that contributed to his undoing. A mercenary and deceitful spirit is suggested by his criticism of Mary's anointing of Jesus' feet with expensive unguent, saying its value could have been better used. John puts this baldly: Judas "was a thief, and as he had the money box he used to take what was put into it."

> Mine own Apostle, who the bag did bear,
> Though he had all I had, did not forbear

To sell me also, and to put me there —
    Was ever grief like mine?

For thirty pence he did my death devise,
Who at three hundred did the ointment prize,
Not half so sweet as my sweet sacrifice —
    Was ever grief like mine?
                    (George Herbert [1593–1633], "The Sacrifice")

The immediate mention of Judas' resolution to betray, following upon Jesus' reference to his coming *burial* (Matt. 26:12, 14), has also suggested a thwarted personal ambition, which could not accept frustration by Jesus' death. This is somewhat confirmed by Judas' acceptance of a bribe for betraying Jesus, as though to salvage some reward from the ruin of his hopes.

The most frequent description of Judas as one "who also betrayed . . . who became a traitor" emphasizes his personal responsibility for what happened. We are told he "was a devil," that "Satan entered into him," that "the devil put it into the heart of Judas to betray him"; but never so as to exonerate Judas from blame. It was commonly believed that demonic power took control only of hearts willing to cooperate, of minds that gave entrance and consent to implanted evil. Luke, accordingly, mentions the satanic origin of the betrayal, Judas' acceptance of money, and his *seeking* of opportunity all in one sentence.

That Judas became the tool of purposes larger than he understood is clear; but that he was not helpless, but was a willing collaborator, is also clear. He did what he did because he wanted to, not because he was "fated" to do so. The accepted bribe and the kiss within the garden expose the hardened heart of Judas beyond excuse.

Knowing all, and taking due precautions, Jesus included Judas within the group for the final meal. The gulf between Judas and Jesus had widened; criticism of others' devotion, and common pilfering, had now given place to resistance, loss of confidence in Jesus, and active conspiracy. Judas awaits his opportunity — but it is Jesus who acts.

With infinite gentleness, even yet affording Judas his protection, not forcing him into irrevocable decision, Jesus nevertheless brought the situation to a head. "Truly, truly, I say to you, one of you will betray me" conveys clear warning. Judas cannot hide his real purpose any longer, either from Jesus or from himself. Peter's whispered request to the "beloved disciple," who was reclining at the low table with his head nearest to Christ's, to discover of whom Jesus was speaking, was answered equally quietly, "It is he to whom I shall give this morsel when I have dipped it." And Jesus offered the choice tidbit, the courtesy shown by a host toward a favored guest — to Judas.

> But when from out the dish the sop he drew
>   Which to the traitor his dark soul betrayed,
> All bitterness from all the herbs that grew
>   Since man lost paradise, that sop conveyed.
>
> (Anonymous [c. 1856], "The Sop")

It was a final, veiled appeal that must have seared Judas' conscience, a moment of truth and destiny. But Judas hardened his heart, and "*Satan* entered *into* him." Jesus at once spoke the decisive word of expulsion and of judgment: "What you are going to do, do quickly." Judas immediately went out; and in every sense "it was night."

"Now no one at the table knew why Jesus said this to him," or for that matter what the giving of the morsel implied. They speculated that perhaps Judas had gone to buy things needed for the feast, or to give the required Passover alms to the poor. Had the Eleven understood, who can say what violent action they might have taken? But Jesus forestalls any intervention, accepting his own peril, protecting Judas.

Nevertheless, Judas is expelled. The group upon which the future depended was cleansed by an act of self-exclusion that was yet an act of judgment. Jesus will have more to say on that a little later.

Jesus' Reactions

The closing of the door behind Judas strikes for Jesus the hour that throughout John's Gospel has been anticipated. Jesus reacts in two quite unexpected ways.

First, he speaks of glory. Neither angry nor embittered, Jesus calmly accepts, and announces, the end that awaits him. With Judas' departure the future is settled, unchangeable, as good as accomplished: "Now is the Son of man glorified. . . ." The words echo similar expressions earlier in the Gospel, all referring to the fulfillment of God's purpose through the death, resurrection, and ascension of Christ. His passion and its sequel were his path to glory: Judas' removal was the first decisive step on that last journey.

"Yet a little while I am with you. You will seek me; and as I said to the Jews so now I say to you, 'Where I am going you cannot come.'" The dread announcement confirms their worst fears. There remain only final explanations, then for him the dark way forward to glory. And this "at once" (v. 32) — all is in the Father's hands.

Christ's second unexpected reaction to the departure of Judas was to urge the "new" commandment, "that you love one another." This is not the ancient Jewish law "You shall love your neighbor as yourself" to which Jesus had earlier lent his own authority. This is a new command for different circumstances, a call for close, unbreakable fidelity between disciples, for what John's Epistle calls "love of the brethren." It has nothing to do with pious sentiment, with Christian "togetherness" and emotional "fellowship." Jesus is calling for solidarity, for closed ranks and steadfast mutual loyalty in the approaching crisis.

Before them all was the sad example of disunity, of defection to the enemy. It had been impossible to call to mutual loyalty while Judas was present: he did not share the special bond that grappled true hearts to Christ in gratitude and love. Jesus is demanding an attitude the opposite to that of Judas, and what he here commands he later prays for: "that they may be one."

Around them lies the watchful, menacing world; ahead is the pressure of persecution. They will need a united front to face the coming years. If disciples do not stand together in the future, there will be no disciples, and no future. Only as they stand together, confronting the world's hatred with unshakable loyalty, will men take note of a new quality of brotherhood in the earth, and recognize that they are Christ's kind of men: "By this all men will know that you are my disciples, if you have love for one another."

So indeed it happened. Finding it impossible to use one Christian against another, or to divide Christian from Christian by bribes or threats, persecutors did come to exclaim (as Tertullian records, *Apology* 39:7), "See how these Christians love one another . . . how they are ready to die for each other."

47

"As I have loved you": the background to the charge was the disciples' experience of Christ's steadfast, unbreakable loyalty to them. In spite of their slowness, their mistakes and fears, Jesus has (as John has said) "loved his own which were in the world," and he "loved them to the end." It was no mere affectionate admiration for the lovable, the dependable, the mature; it was a patient, understanding, and forgiving loyalty that ever dealt faithfully with their faults, yet washed their feet, and would stand by them through all the testing future of pressure and persecution. Such was to be the quality of their loyalty to each other.

Glory and love: so Jesus reacted to the departure of one of the Twelve to serve his foes. Jesus would revert also to this theme, but the immediate moment was tense, and his own thought was interrupted (in the record as we now have it) by the reaction of the Eleven with an outburst of questions — "Who? Where? Why, Lord?"

Meanwhile, Judas sped through the darkened streets to join the enemy, his heart hardened against his Lord, his life closed against his golden opportunity, out into the loneliness of a sin he could never live with, into the shadows of a night that would end in self-destruction. For

> . . . he that shuts Love out, in turn shall be
> Shut out from Love, and on her threshold lie
> Howling, in outer darkness.
>
> (Alfred, Lord Tennyson [1809–1892],
> "To — —" [Introduction to Palace of Art])

"As they were eating, he said, 'Truly, I say to you, one of you will betray me.' And they were very sorrowful, and began to say to him one after another, 'Is it I, Lord?'"

> Someone is slighting the Saviour of men —
> Lord, is it I?
> Someone is spurning his love once again —
> Lord, is it I?
> Someone is living in selfish delight:
> Lord, is it I?

Someone is turning his face from the light —
    Lord, is it I?
Someone's betraying his Master today:
    Lord, is it I?
Someone is walking a perilous way —
    Lord, is it I?

(J. R. Clements)

Bewildered
Conversation

7:
"Who? Where? Why?"

JOHN 13:21–30, 36–14:4

When Jesus had thus spoken, he was troubled in spirit, and testified, "Truly, truly, I say to you, one of you will betray me." The disciples looked at one another, uncertain of whom he spoke. One of his disciples, whom Jesus loved, was lying close to the breast of Jesus; so Simon Peter beckoned to him and said, "Tell us who it is of whom he speaks." So lying thus, close to the breast of Jesus, he said to him, "Lord, who is it?" Jesus answered, "It is he to whom I shall give this morsel when I have dipped it." So when he had dipped the morsel, he gave it to Judas, the son of Simon Iscariot. Then after the morsel, Satan entered into him. Jesus said to him, "What you are going to do, do quickly." Now no one at the table knew why he said this to him. Some thought that, because Judas had the money box, Jesus was telling him, "Buy what we need for the feast"; or, that he should give something to the poor. So, after receiving the morsel, he immediately went out; and it was night.

Simon Peter said to him, "Lord, where are you going?" Jesus answered, "Where I am going you cannot follow me now; but you shall follow afterward." Peter said to him, "Lord, why cannot I follow you now? I will lay down my life for you." Jesus answered, "Will you lay down your life for me? Truly, truly, I say to you, the cock will not crow, till you have denied me three times.

"Let not your hearts be troubled; believe in God, believe also in me. In my Father's house are many rooms; if it were not so, would I have told you that I go to prepare a place for you? And when I go and prepare a place for you, I will come again and will take you to myself, that where I am you may be also. And you know the way where I am going."

WITH the departure of Judas from the upper room, action gave place to a buzz of conversation, and especially to rapid questions and replies. The immediate inquiries of the "beloved disciple" ("Lord, who . . . ?"), of Peter ("Lord, where . . . ?", "Lord, why . . . ?"), of Thomas ("Lord, how . . . ?"); Philip's request ("Lord, show us . . ."), and the plea of the "other" Judas ("Lord, how is it . . . ?") illustrate vividly the doubts, perplexities, and fears stirred in the Eleven by the solemn words of Jesus, and by actions they do not understand.

The questions are simple in form, but the atmosphere, the circumstances, and the answers that Jesus gave add profound implications to each inquiry. A curiously oblique, or indirect, manner of reply is noticeable in John's Gospel. For example, "Rabbi, where are you staying?" is answered by an invitation to a protracted interview, as though the question really meant, "Rabbi, may we visit and consult with you?" (1:38f.). Nicodemus' opening remark, "Rabbi, we know that you are a teacher come from God . . ." is cut short with "Unless one is born anew, he cannot see the kingdom of God," as though the remark were leading up to some such question as, "What have you to offer that is not written in the law?" Again, the query, "Are there not twelve hours in the day?" turns out to carry the reassuring implication that the man of God is always safe until his work is done.

Jesus replies to the unspoken thought, the half-expressed intention, rather than to the immediate question. So when Peter asked, "Lord, where are you going?" Jesus replied, "You cannot follow me now." Each instance requires careful attention.

1. Upon Jesus' announcement that "One of you will betray me," "the disciple whom Jesus loved" inquired, "Lord, who is it?" Everyone wishes to know the identity of the disciple who asked this question. Probably the best available guess is that he was John the son of Zebedee, though the argument that supports it is extraordinarily complicated and full of assumptions very difficult to prove. It can be said with equal conviction that any disciple could call himself "beloved," and that no disciple would dare call himself "the" disciple whom Jesus loved. Some therefore think the writer was talking about himself, others that he could not be! Some, again, find it significant that in 11:5 the author plainly tells us that Jesus loved *Lazarus*, and only after that "introduction" does he refer to "the disciple whom Jesus loved." But why not use the name Lazarus? And was Lazarus

present in the upper room? It is usually taken for granted (another assumption!) that only the Twelve were there with Jesus.

Whoever it was, the disciple whom Jesus loved was trusted with the first clear hint of who would betray Jesus, though still in the ambiguous form of the favored guest's portion, which no one (even the beloved disciple) understood (13:23–28). It is surely significant that, despite the trust and the love, none of the disciples could be given a plain, unequivocal, ready-made answer when each asked "Is it I?"

John explains that Peter instigated the inquiry; Matthew says that others, including Judas Iscariot, "began to say to him one after another, 'Is it I, Lord?' " Evidently the uneasiness and self-distrust were general. John says that Jesus answered the beloved disciple, evidently whispering to one so close to him, "It is he to whom I shall give this morsel when I have dipped it," and gave the portion to Judas. Matthew records that Jesus replied to Judas' own question, "Is it I, Master?" with the words "You have said so."

Why was it left thus uncertain — on the one hand, none knowing why Judas left (v. 28), not even Judas himself given a clear "Yes, you!", and on the other hand, no one given the firm assurance, "No, it is not you"? Is it not because such a question must always be answered, in the end, by each for himself? We follow Jesus, or we betray him, as we choose, and at our own peril.

2. Peter, however, is arrested by that strange remark, which threatened the separation he most dreaded: "You will seek me; and as I said to the Jews so now I say to you, 'Where I am going you cannot come.' " What can this mean? Had not Jesus from the beginning called them to follow him? Peter desired above all things to stay with Jesus — to whom else could he go, when Jesus had the words of eternal life? "I will lay down my life for you." Hence his perplexed "Lord, where are you going?" implying, to judge from Jesus' reply, "Wherever it is, I am coming with you!"

We must admire that passionate, though uncomprehending, doggedness of intention. And Jesus replied, first, to that implication: "Where I am going you cannot follow me now, but you shall follow afterward." The distinction of time is important. As to "now," Peter is totally unready; he does not know the frailty of his own best resolves. Impulsive gestures do very well — as gestures; they do not make for strong, consistent discipleship. Impulsiveness is discouraged in all the Gospels. Jesus would always have his followers "sit down first," reckon up their resources, measure their promises, count the cost.

3. The unspoken thought surfaces in Peter's second question, "Lord, why cannot I follow you now? I will lay down my life for you." Jesus must answer faithfully, and Peter must come to know himself. Superficial commitments must be tested to be proved. According to Luke, the warning ran, "Simon, Simon, behold, Satan demanded to have you, that he might sift you like wheat, but I have prayed for you that your faith may not fail; and when you have turned again, strengthen your brethren." Jesus does not pray that Peter may evade the test, or that he might be delivered from it. The sifting must be faced — though the outcome is hopeful.

John's recollection preserves sterner words, both factual and uncompromising. To Peter's protest "I will lay down my life for you," Jesus answered bluntly that before the night was through, Peter to save his own skin will three times deny that he ever knew Christ. It was all too clear that Peter could not follow "now." Poor Peter! He does not speak, or appear, again in John until 18:15 — the story of the denial. Did Jesus' words shock him into silence? The question "Why cannot I follow now?" often has a sadly self-revealing, humbling answer. But finding the truth about ourselves, and accepting it, forges character.

For "afterward" Peter *will* follow, and to martyrdom. Jesus knew his man, and when Peter by the fire at the lakeside retraced his denials, Jesus had no doubt of his ultimate loyalty. Nor does he doubt the Eleven. The pronouns become plural as he speaks again to all, and the tone of his speech changes. They must not despair, either because of the world's hostility or because of their own frailty. In the end they shall arrive, together, at the Father's house. Nothing will be lost, nothing is in doubt, the future is in his hands. Therefore they must take their own hearts under discipline, and *not let* them be troubled. Instead, they must hold fast to the God they know, and to the Lord they have so far trusted.

In this way Jesus replies, secondly, to the question itself, "Lord, where are you going?" The words of peace and assurance seem out of place following so solemn a warning, until we notice that Jesus returns to the surface meaning of the question and addresses the Eleven together. The direct answer to "Lord, where . . .?" is one of the best-known and best-loved passages in the Gospels. Though the translation is debatable, as the varied versions show, yet the general meaning is clear.

The Father's House

These famous verses had no direct reference, originally, to the Christian's death. They describe Christ's "destination" as he leaves this life. But it is hardly surprising that they find a place in every definition of the Christian hope, and in nearly every Christian funeral service. Simple, and familiar, the words seem at first sight to say little about life beyond death. But what is said is precious, and probably sufficient.

1. *Death is returning home.* "The Father's house" is used in 2:16 for the Jerusalem temple, as in Mark 11:17 — "My house shall be called a house of prayer. . . ." But to Jewish hearts the temple was essentially the place where God *dwelt.* In protest against an exaggerated reverence for the place, some insisted that the eternal God "does not dwell in houses made with hands," as though confined there, imprisoned, and kept (as were idols) from interfering in daily life. But the original promise, repeated endlessly in the Old Testament, was that Israel's God would "dwell among them," unlike the gods of Greece, too remote to care, or the gods of Edom, Moab, and the rest, safely aloof on mountaintops or in desert places.

The shrine was, to simple piety, God's home among his people, as indeed God himself was, to deepest thought, man's eternal home — "our dwelling-place in all generations." Jeremiah has a moving picture of the souls of men and women, fashioned to turn homeward like migrating birds, by an instinct old as humanity, "homing" upon God (8:7).

"The house of God" is thus more than an ornate sanctuary, though wherever God dwells, worship occurs. The "house" is home, and dwelling-place, and resting place with God, eternity made familiar and satisfying. "More home-like seems the vast unknown" since Jesus precedes us there, and hosts of those "loved long since and lost awhile," awaiting reunion

When that which drew from out the boundless deep
Turns again *home*.

(Alfred, Lord Tennyson [1809–1892], "Crossing the Bar")

2. *There is abundant room* — a statement of faith, not of imagination. "In my Father's house are many rooms" seems intended to assure that none need be shut out: there is room for all who would come. Literally, "room" means a place to stay, "abiding-place"; the word is used in verse 23 for "home," "dwelling-place."

"Many mansions" (AV/KJV) arose from the word "mansio" in the Latin versions, meaning an inn, a camp for the night. To English ears, this translation hopelessly distorts the meaning by suggesting luxury, pomp, and grandeur. In Latin it gave rise to the thought of progress in heaven from one "stopping place," bivouac, camp-for-the-night to the next. More probably the background is Jewish, the idea of many compartments in Sheol, and the intention simply to emphasize that there is room for all who make the pilgrimage.

3. *There will be welcome.* As two disciples had gone ahead that day to prepare the upper room for the evening meal, so Jesus, as host, "goes before to prepare a place"; the language is that of simple hospitality, of loving preparation for welcome guests.

It is difficult not to think here of Stephen's vision of Christ *standing* at the right hand of God to receive Stephen's soul to glory, or to recall the Psalmist's expression of exactly the same thought, that God who is shepherd and guide throughout our life will be our host at the end:

Thou preparest a table before me in the presence of mine
    enemies;
  thou anointest my head with oil, my cup overflows.
Surely goodness and mercy shall follow me [Moffatt: shall
    wait upon me]
  all the days of my life;
  and I shall dwell in the house of the Lord for ever.

A place was prepared for Christ as he went to the Father, and he promises the same for his own: "I will come again and take you to myself." Though they cannot follow immediately, for his vicarious, expiating death must be unshared, yet they will follow eventually, and he will come to meet them.

What a high favour's this,
That God should be man's harbinger to bliss!
When John prepared the way before Thy face,
O Christ, 'twas no small grace
Unto the Baptist then;
Much greater dost Thou now bestow on men,
In that Thou goest before to make us room
In heaven against we come.

(Thomas Washbourne [1606–1687], "I go to prepare a place for
you")

4. *There will be fellowship.* Even heaven could not be "home"
otherwise, but Jesus spells it out — "that where I am you may be
also." Imagination fails to create the pictures we long for, depicting that afterlife; exactly as imagination failed to provide us
in the womb with any pictures of life in that busy world — of
men, color, light, sound, and love — that did nevertheless await
us at birth. What cannot be imagined is still *real*, and concerning
that other existence we are sufficiently assured of personal survival ("eternal life"), recognition (else existence would sink to
impersonal levels), love ("which abides"), and fellowship with
God, with Christ, with the Spirit, and with each other (since
without fellowship love is meaningless). All this we know because we have known God: the roots of the hope of immortality
lie in the total religious experience. "It is not in heaven that we
shall find God, but in God that we find heaven."

Not spilt like water on the ground,
Not wrapt in dreamless sleep profound,
Not wandering in unknown despair
Beyond Thy voice, Thine arm, Thy care;
Not left to lie like fallen tree:
Not dead, but living unto Thee.

O Giver unto man of breath,
O Holder of the keys of death,
O Quickener of the life within,
Save us from death, the death of sin;
That body, soul, and spirit be
For ever living unto Thee.

(John Ellerton [1826–1893], "God of the Living")

Through all the coming darkness and storm, they need not then be troubled. Around them is the threatening world; just ahead, the dreaded loss of Christ's physical presence; within, their frequent misgivings, self-accusation, and fears; beyond, probable suffering, possible martyrdom. But at the end, rendezvous will be kept in the Father's home. Neither Judas, nor Pilate, nor Caiaphas, nor Caesar, nor the prince of this world will be able to frustrate that sure hope of reunion. It is built upon his faithfulness — "If it were not so would I have told you that I go to prepare a place for you?" That cannot change. Besides, they now know whither he goes, and the way there.

Or do they?

Poor Peter! But am I ready to perform one half of what I promise? Show me myself . . .

> *Show me myself, O holy Lord;*
>   *Help me to look within;*
> *I will not turn me from the sight*
>   *Of all my sin.*
>
> *Not mine the life I thought to live*
>   *When first I took His name;*
> *Mine but the right to weep and grieve*
>   *Over my shame.*
>
> *Yet, Lord, I thank Thee for the sight*
>   *Thou hast vouchsafed to me;*
> *And humbled to the dust I shrink*
>   *Closer to Thee.*
>
> *And if Thy love will not disown*
>   *So frail a heart as mine,*
> *Chasten and cleanse it as Thou wilt —*
>   *But keep it Thine!*

(Anonymous, in Plymouth Hymnal [Brooklyn, N.Y.], 1893)

A brave prayer.

8:
"How Can We Know the Way?"

JOHN 14:3-7

"And when I go and prepare a place for you, I will come again and will take you to myself, that where I am you may be also. And you know the way where I am going." Thomas said to him, "Lord, we do not know where you are going; how can we know the way?" Jesus said to him, "I am the way, and the truth, and the life; no one comes to the Father, but by me. If you had known me, you would have known my Father also; henceforth you know him and have seen him."

THE fourth quick-fire question is from Thomas, provoked by Christ's assertion that the Eleven knew where he was going, and the way. "Lord," Thomas protested, "we do not know where you are going; how can we know the way?" Doubtless Thomas' earnest perplexity made the contradiction sound ruder than he intended, but the sadness and seriousness of the moment made the question urgent.

For Thomas is not merely repeating Peter's inquiry about Jesus' destination. That had been answered: "the Father's house." Jesus' profound reply to Thomas makes clear that the question asked more; and so does all we know of Thomas.

Although Thomas has little place in the other Gospels, being a mere name within a list, he holds crucial importance in John. Earlier, he emerged as spokesman for the disciples in Bethany-beyond-Jordan, when on receiving news of Lazarus' death Jesus proposed to return to Judea. The disciples protest at the danger, but when Jesus insists, Thomas responds with dogged, if despairing, loyalty: "Let us also go, that we may die with him."

Later, Thomas' doubts on Easter Day crystallize the main problem John is dealing with; that is, how men and women come to faith. In consequence, Thomas' glorious capitulation, "My Lord, and my God," forms the true climax to John's Gospel, and earns the blessing pronounced on all those who "see not, yet believe." Thomas, in fact, is central to John's whole argument.

A Far-searching Question

Here, it is Thomas again who asks the all-important question that is in all their minds, "What of the future?" He is thinking both about Jesus' immediate departure and about the wholly changed, frightening way ahead without the Lord. "What now? Where do we go from here?" It is to that underlying anxiety about the way forward that Jesus replies.

In the remote background of Thomas' question may lie the familiar Jewish notion of "the way of the Lord" in which the godly "walk," the pilgrimage led by fire and cloud, the Way appointed in the Torah as the will of God for life. The same idea prompted the earliest description of Christianity as "the Way," and of followers of Jesus as "people of the Way," signifying the Christian life-style, or way of living. Nearer to Thomas' mind, no doubt, was the thought of future days without the instruction, the daily example and inspiration, of Jesus; days demanding, dangerous, and leaderless. "How can *we* know the way?" How can we be sure of arriving safe, at last, within the Father's house?

But the same longing finds expression, again and again, far beyond the Christian circle. In lines attributed to "M. Farrow," for example, we feel poignantly the "lostness" of humanity:

> Give us wills of steel
> And be our magnetic pole.
> Draw us unwavering through the wastes
> Whence the signs of salvation are vanishing.
> Thou art our Journey's End
> (Give us wills of steel!).
> The world has forgotten its home
> And the things that belong to its peace.
> If our compass fail
> Our footsteps stagger and reel,
> And all our marchings nothing avail
> But to bring us back on ourselves in circles,
> In dizzying, nightmare, maniac rings
> From whence is no release.

Draw us home . . .
The world is lost, and is looking for the way.

([M. Farrow], "Prayer from the Brink")

"The world is lost, and is looking for the way." Thomas may not have had this universal cry in mind, but the answer Jesus makes reaches far beyond the immediate situation in the upper room and speaks with sharp relevance to a time like our own. Today, so very many have lost the clue to life's meaning — when moral leadership is almost bankrupt, when statesmanship descends to mere struggle for power, when God's church is voiceless, and when the very Scripture seems dissolving into individual taste among many conflicting versions; when "conscience" has receded into individual convenience.

Into such bleak confusion, Jesus' words drop with heart-exciting assurance: "I AM THE WAY. . . ."

A Tremendous Answer

Christ's reply to Thomas adds yet further self-manifestation to the evening's revelations. He is himself the way that men must walk; the way that men must believe — "the truth"; and the way that men must live — "the life." He is the disciples' only hope of ever finding their way through the hostile world and the unknowable future: he is also humankind's only hope of ever finding the way to the Father, which is the way home. "No one comes to the Father, but by me."

The unfathomable utterance recalls the Old Testament description of God as "our dwelling-place," our origin, home, and destination. It recalls, too, warnings like "There is a way which seems right to a man, but its end is the way to death" (Prov. 14:12), and prayers like "Make me to know thy ways, O Lord; teach me thy paths" (Psalm 25:4). But at the same time it asserts that the way forward, the way home, the way to God is neither the ancient law, nor the tradition of the elders, nor yet some abstract pattern of morality or piety inherited within religious culture: the way is Christ himself. He is the direction, and the path, and the guide, to humankind's true destiny.

Literally translated, Christ's reply was "I am the way, and the truth, and the life" — a *threefold* claim. But the question was concerning the "way," and the added words about coming to the

Father "by me" also focus upon the "way." Hence the familiar translation, "I am the true and living way" — a *single* claim. It is impossible to be dogmatic about which translation better represents the original, but the difference is not great. Jesus means that he is the appointed way of behavior, of belief, and of being; the focus of faith, the pathfinder blazing the trail.

A medieval writer represents Jesus explaining his own words:

> Without the way which I have opened, thou canst not return to paradise; without the truth which I communicate, thou canst not know the way; without the life which I quicken, thou canst not obey the truth. I am the way which thou must go, the truth which thou must believe, and the life which thou must desire and hope for — the invariable and perfect way, the supreme and infallible truth, the blessed, uncreated, endless life.
>
> (Thomas a Kempis [1379–1471], *Imitation of Christ* [III.xlii.1 in
> John Payne's translation])

We of the twentieth century, who commonly seek our way forward, and even our way home to God, in books, moral codes, private conscience or reason, science, mysticism, visions and ecstasies, psychology, gurus, an infallible church, or the stars, may place beside á Kempis a comment of our time:

> The path we have to follow is a narrow one. It runs all the time on the edge of a precipitous mystery, sometimes taking you up to the sunlit heights and the Mount of Transfiguration, and sometimes taking you down into the fires of suffering and into the shadow of death. Following Christ means, that when you find these dizzy things before you, these dark things in your path, you go through them and not round them. . . . Easy enough when the road runs by the shining shores of the lake of Galilee, but not so easy when it runs into the garden of Gethsemane and becomes the *via dolorosa*.
>
> (L. P. Jacks [1860–1955])

Yet even that does not exhaust the range of meaning in "I am the way. . . ." For it is Christ himself, and not merely the pattern of his life, who is the true and living path to God. To tread the "way" is to love, believe, obey, imitate, and draw life from him. It is to let him lead us, in living experience, to God. That is clearly implied in the sad postscript to the tremendous claim:

"If you had known me, you would have known my Father also; henceforth you know him and have seen him."

That is the heart of Jesus' reply to Thomas: the way forward, the way home, the way to the Father — one way — lies in knowing God through Christ. "He shall be to thee better than light": the way of God to guide our feet, the truth of God to illumine our minds, the life of God within the soul — all *are ours* in Christ. These will lead, through every waiting experience, surely and safely on to God.

So Jesus promised. But what, in plain terms, in practical experience, does that *mean*? So Philip demanded.

> *A stranger here, as all my fathers were*
> *That went before, I wander to and fro;*
> *From earth to heaven is my pilgrimage,*
> *A tedious way for flesh and blood to go.*
> *O Thou that art the way, pity the blind*
> *And teach me how I may Thy dwelling find. . . .*
>
> (Anonymous [15th–16th century])

> *We think we must climb to a certain height of goodness*
> *before we can reach God. But He says, not "At the*
> *end of the way you may find me"; He says "I am the*
> *Way; I am the road under your feet, the road that*
> *begins just as low down as you happen to be. . . ."*
> *The moment we turn to walk in the way we are*
> *walking in God. The moment we set our face in the*
> *same direction as His, we are walking with God.*
>
> (Helen Wodehouse, "Nights and Days")

9:
"What is God Really Like?"

JOHN 14:6-21

Jesus said to him, "I am the way, and the truth, and the life; no one comes to the Father, but by me. If you had known me, you would have known my Father also; henceforth you know him and have seen him."

Philip said to him, "Lord, show us the Father, and we shall be satisfied." Jesus said to him, "Have I been with you so long, and yet you do not know me, Philip? He who has seen me has seen the Father; how can you say, 'Show us the Father'? Do you not believe that I am in the Father and the Father in me? The words that I say to you I do not speak on my own authority; but the Father who dwells in me does his works. Believe me that I am in the Father and the Father in me; or else believe me for the sake of the works themselves.

"Truly, truly, I say to you, he who believes in me will also do the works that I do; and greater works than these will he do, because I go to the Father. Whatever you ask in my name, I will do it, that the Father may be glorified in the Son; if you ask anything in my name, I will do it.

"If you love me, you will keep my commandments. And I will pray the Father, and he will give you another Counselor, to be with you for ever, even the Spirit of truth, whom the world cannot receive, because it neither sees him nor knows him; you know him, for he dwells with you, and will be in you.

"I will not leave you desolate; I will come to you. Yet a little while, and the world will see me no more, but you will see me; because I live, you will live also. In that day you will know that I am in my Father, and you in me, and I in you. He who has my commandments and keeps them, he it is who loves me; and he who loves me will be loved by my Father, and I will love him and manifest myself to him."

FOR the second time Christ's answer to one disciple provokes a further question from another, this time from Philip, and this time, also, the most probing and profound question of all. Seizing swiftly upon the words, "If you had known me you would have known my Father also; henceforth you know him . . . ," Philip pleads, "Lord, show us the Father, and we shall be satisfied," implying, at least, that we shall "ask no more" (NEB).

If in Thomas' question "How can we know the way?" we hear the longing of a lost world, in Philip's we feel the urgent, deep desire of the truly religious soul, "Show me God: tell me what God is really like."

That plea has special significance for John, who has insisted twice (1:18; 6:46) that "No one has ever seen God," and (probably) says it yet again in his Epistle (4:12); and who makes the self-manifestation of Jesus as representative, Servant, and transparent incarnation of God his chief theme. No one has seen God, *but we have seen Christ.*

The question might well have special significance for Philip, also. He too is little more than a name in the other Gospels, yet he becomes in John a distinct personality, and an attractive, intriguing one. The little we know suggests an earnest, deeply thoughtful disciple. His name is Greek, just possibly hinting at a wider-than-Jewish background; and to him came certain Greeks in Jerusalem who desired to see Jesus. He appears (in John 1) to be the only recruit whom Jesus himself sought out, and he in turn brought to Jesus another very earnest and thoughtful follower, Nathanael.

At the feeding of the five thousand, according to John, Jesus asked Philip "How are we to buy bread . . . ?" This he said "to test him," and received a prosaic, calculating, and negative reply: "Two hundred pence would not buy enough. . . ." Since nothing came of the "test," it is permissible to ask if Jesus were in fact teasing his serious, thoughtful, very anxious disciple!

Here in the upper room, Philip has followed the drift of Christ's meaning, sees the problems that will be created by his departure, and fastens upon the essence of the situation and the central need of the future — to be sure of God. To know the way forward they must know God. So Philip would press Christ further on his challenging reply to Thomas, "How are we to be so sure of God?"

That is the voice of the earnest heart, longing for certainty, assurance, and hope, craving to be satisfied in God. Philip's is no idly speculative question, no mere invitation to theological discussion. With the rest, he feels the tenseness of the moment, the menace of the future; his down-to-earth nature desires no mystic obscurities but a plain and practical assurance that Christ's God will remain with them. *"Show* us the Father . . ." — and we shall be all right!

Beyond and beneath the "hunger for meaning," the "hunt for certainties," the instinct for immortality, the consciousness of moral duty, the wonder evoked by creation's beauty and order, and the enrichment that comes from fellowship and from Scripture, the religious spirit yearns for immediate and individual awareness of God, at least occasionally. John's contemporaries felt this the more keenly as the eyewitnesses to God's presence in Christ were passing away. Glowing memories from second-hand sources were no substitute for "an existential experience of the divine." For them, as for ourselves, Philip's "Show *us* the Father . . ." had poignant overtones, and Jesus' reply a permanent relevance.

Timeless Revelation

To so earnest a request, no slick and superficial answer could be offered. Jesus begins, again a little sadly and reproachfully, with what they already should have known: "Have I been with you so long, and yet you do not know me, Philip?" and continues with a truly astonishing assertion: "He who has seen me has seen the Father; how can you say, 'Show us the Father'? Do you not believe that I am in the Father and the Father in me?"

The way to know God is — first — *to know Jesus.* The assertion of the mutual indwelling of Father and Son is spelled out in the plainest way: "the words that I say to you I do not speak on my own authority . . . the Father who dwells in me does his works." Put another way, if it is the Father's words you desire to hear, then listen to Jesus; if it is the Father's actions you wish to see, watch Jesus; if it is the Father's presence you long for, come to Jesus. "Believe me that I am in the Father and the Father in me."

John insists that as no one comes to the Father but by Christ, so no one can know the Father save through him, and this remains true for subsequent generations. He himself is writing Christ's story that this may be known to those who were not there. Though he does not record the instituting of the Lord's supper, he is certainly aware that the Lord's table keeps alive in the church the memory of Jesus. Presently John will lay great emphasis on the presence in the church of the Spirit to bring all things to remembrance.

Thus, though some — highly privileged — could say,

> That which was from the beginning, which we have heard, which we have seen with our eyes, which we have looked upon and touched with our hands . . . that which we have seen and heard we proclaim . . .

yet the eyewitnessed revelation of God in Christ was not confined to the first century. Scripture, sacrament, and the Spirit preserve the story and its meaning for all generations, and the first step for any earnest seeker after God must be attentive and openhearted reading of the Gospels with the assurance of Jesus in mind — "he who has seen me has seen the Father."

Yet, precious and essential though such means to the knowledge of God must ever be, *it is still secondhand.* Even for those in the upper room that means of knowing God would soon become a memory. What means of knowing God *at firsthand* would remain for them and — equally important — for John's contemporaries? What means still remain for us, who were born too late, when our hearts cry "Show us the Father"?

Simply, and plainly, Jesus replies: believing — working — praying — and loving obedience.

1. "Believe me that I am in the Father and the Father in me; or else believe me for the sake of the works themselves." Faith, for John, is never wishful thinking — there are situations and moods when *not* to believe in God would accord more with our wishes! Faith is instead a kind of insight, a way of "seeing," without which men and women remain "blind," living in darkness even in the presence of the light of the world. Some spiritual discernment, some desire, ability, and patience, to see beneath the material surface of life is plainly requisite to even the shallowest knowledge of God.

2. "He who believes in me will also do the works that I do; and greater works than these will he do, because I go to the Father." It is misleading to think of Christ's "works" as simply his miracles, for John regularly uses another word for them.

"Works" include general behavior, deeds (3:20f.), divine activity of all kinds (5:20), and all that Jesus accomplished (5:26). Into this "work" the disciple must enter: the knowledge of God is never a matter of intellect or of idle contemplation, but requires involvement in God's concern, commitment to God's cause.

What precisely was intended by the "greater works" that the Eleven would do is harder to say. From the perspective of John's hindsight, long after Christ had "gone to the Father," the enormous geographical, racial, and spiritual expansion of the Christian movement would certainly be part of the apostolic experience of God. Doubtless that was part, at least, of what Jesus meant.

3. "Whatever you ask in my name, I will do it, that the Father may be glorified in the Son; if you ask anything in my name, I will do it." The Eleven, and subsequent generations, will know the Father in a prayer experience of a wholly new quality. No unlimited guarantee is offered here, that every stray desire lifted to God along with Christ's name as a kind of charm or spell will be fulfilled. The clearly implied limitations add weight to the promise: when we ask things worthy of putting Christ's name to, things that will truly glorify the Father (v. 13), then Christ undertakes to grant what we request. To prayer on that level of confidence and submission, God will certainly make himself known.

4. And the love that keeps Christ's commandments will know God, too:

> If you love me, you will keep my commandments. And I will pray the Father, and he will give you another Counselor. . . . He who has my commandments and keeps them, he it is who loves me; and he who loves me will be loved by my Father, and I will love him and manifest myself to him.

John is far too realistic to talk about "love for Jesus" in an emotional way: in his Gospel and Epistle, love is always closely associated with obedience, or (as here) defined in terms of obedience. Obedience without love is not Christian devotion but resentful or fearful submission; "love" without obedience would be mere sentiment, or self-delusion. Loving obedience is the attitude entirely appropriate for the redeemed believer toward his Savior and Lord. To one living in that attitude, the promise is clear: he or she will know God by the Spirit, know God in his unchanging love, and know Christ in fullness.

In such belief — work — prayer — love — obedience is summarized the essence of every individual Christian experience: to him who so believes, works, asks, loves, and obeys, Christ promises that the Father will come and make himself known. In this way, what at first sight appear to be detached sayings of Jesus (vv. 11–15) added to the reply to Philip, prove to be strictly relevant to what Philip asked. Even so, faith, work, prayer, and loving obedience do not "discover" God — they are conditions, not channels, of revelation. It is God himself who comes, by the Spirit (vv. 16–19, to which we will return), to make himself known. That is why, as we see at the close of this analysis of Christian experience after his "departure," Jesus returns directly to Philip's request: "Yet a little while, and the world will see me no more, but you will see me; because I live, you will live also. *In that day, you will know* that I am in my Father, and you in me, and I in you." "Because I live": the secret of life now, and forever!

The answer to "*Show* us the Father . . ." is, strictly speaking, the promise of fellowship, of indwelling. The coming to the Christian of the Father (v. 23), the Son (v. 18), and the Spirit (v. 16) is stated as three aspects of one divine indwelling, rather than three distinguishable experiences; and in such intimate fellowship with the living God, the second answer to Philip's question is assured. No longer need the heart cry "Show us the Father," for (as Jeremiah promised) "all shall know God, from the least unto the greatest." Though not, indeed, all people: "the world will see me no more"; it is possible only to the person who has the commandments, keeps them, and so loves the Lord.

If Philip's question was profound, the answer he received is richer than he could have anticipated. God may be known, in every generation, at firsthand, by the outward observation of Christ and by the inward experience of faith, work, prayer, love, and obedience. "God was in Christ," and Christ comes to us in the cradle of the Word, as Luther said. For earnest, honest, wakeful readers of the Gospels, Christ still leaves the printed page to "walk up and down in our hearts." And he who so sees Christ sees the Father. But all must "come alive" in ongoing Christian experience if the truth is to kindle into life, and God is to be met, and grasped, and worshiped — as well as talked about.

Again, Jesus has more to say — on prayer, and on the Spirit — before the evening is through; but his answer to Philip is clear and timeless: "You say 'Show us the Father'? — look at me, and live in God."

When did I last experience the immediate awareness of God, an unmistakable sense of his nearness and blessing? Or do I live now upon past recollections and the testimony of others? Do I need to offer Philip's plea — made personal, made urgent? — "Lord, show me the Father, lest I remain always unsatisfied."

10:
"How Only to Us, Lord?"

JOHN 14:20-31

"In that day you will know that I am in my Father, and you in me, and I in you. He who has my commandments and keeps them, he it it is who loves me; and he who loves me will be loved by my Father, and I will love him and manifest myself to him." Judas (not Iscariot) said to him, "Lord, how is it that you will manifest yourself to us, and not to the world?" Jesus answered him, "If a man loves me, he will keep my word, and my Father will love him, and we will come to him and make our home with him. He who does not love me does not keep my words; and the word which you hear is not mine but the Father's who sent me.

"These things I have spoken to you, while I am still with you. But the Counselor, the Holy Spirit, whom the Father will send in my name, he will teach you all things, and bring to your remembrance all that I have said to you. Peace I leave with you; my peace I give to you; not as the world gives do I give to you. Let not your hearts be troubled, neither let them be afraid. You heard me say to you, 'I go away, and I will come to you.' If you loved me, you would have rejoiced, because I go to the Father; for the Father is greater than I. And now I have told you before it takes place, so that when it does take place, you may believe. I will no longer talk much with you, for the ruler of this world is coming. He has no power over me; but I do as the Father has commanded me, so that the world may know that I love the Father. Rise, let us go hence."

SUDDENLY, for the only time in the four Gospels, we hear the voice of the least known of all the disciples, Judas "not Iscariot." He wants to know, "How . . . Lord?"

It is a question often asked in John's Gospel: by Nathanael ("How do you know me?"), by Nicodemus ("How can a man be born when he is old?"), by Jesus of Philip ("How are we to buy bread?"), by the Jews among themselves ("How can this man give us his flesh to eat?"), and by the Jews of the blind man's parents ("How then does he see?"). John illustrates with what varied overtones the question may be put — amazement, incredulity, teasing inquiry, incomprehension, resolute unbelief.

Judas appears to have been left behind in the conversation, but he has caught the promise of some new, exclusive mode of knowing God promised to disciples alone: "Lord, how is it that you will manifest yourself to us, and not to the world?" There is more here than the plain man's impatience with anything mystical or exclusive to a privileged few. Religious zeal far too often makes extravagant claims to esoteric knowledge, a hidden wisdom, private to the initiated. Such claims were common in the groups in which John's Gospel first circulated, and Paul also had to warn the Corinthians against a pride in religious wisdom exclusive to those who could understand "the deep things of God."

Like Paul, who insisted that he was called to teach *every man*, John emphasizes the love of God for *the world*, that whoever believes has eternal life, and (in 1 John) sets up the most rigorous tests by which all such exclusivist claims must be examined. Widespread gnostic sects, both "Christian" and pagan, claimed to know secrets, "mysteries," reserved for the "intellectual," which ordinary believers and the world could never know. Against this background, Judas' question would be remembered as a protest against the kind of intellectual snobbery that the readers met too often. "Lord, how . . . to us and not to the world?"

Jesus' reply had, therefore, a lasting relevance. There is indeed a knowledge of God available to the disciple but not to the world. Yet it is not so much withheld from outsiders, nor intellectually above them, as simply beyond the reach of those not spiritually prepared to receive it. With a hint of sternness, and firmly, as to a slow learner, Jesus repeats what he has just said:

> If a man loves me, he will keep my word, and my Father will love him, and we will come to him and make our home with him. He who does not love me does not keep my words; and the word which you hear is not mine but the Father's who sent me.

73

This is what Jesus had just said to Philip; the repetition and the further restatement in negative form show how important the issue was to John's readers, too.

As the true understanding of music, poetry, visual art, and even pure science is only possible to the specially gifted, so the deepest religious insight — the knowledge of God — is only grasped by those appropriately equipped. But here neither talent, nor temperament, nor intellectual power create the necessary capacity to receive and appreciate the truth: it is a question of loving Christ, keeping his word, being indwelt by God. For God is not to be known as "facts" and "things" are known, by the observation of curious minds; he is known only to those in earnest to understand, to trust, to worship and adore, to accept and surrender.

In biblical terms, to know God implies acquaintance with his ways, experience of his interventions in one's life, openness to every divine approach, readiness for further light and direction. Only the Master would speak of God's then "being at home" in any person's life, but the word well expresses the *rapport* of the godly soul with God and the understanding that results. Once more the simple answer to Judas' question is, "It rests with you!" God is willing to be known and has made himself known, but such knowledge must be spiritually conditioned: the fulfillment of those conditions is in our own hands.

There, for a time, the spate of questions subsided. But (as often happens) this was more because the questioners could think no more than because they were satisfied that all was clear. The future remains unwelcoming and confused; the disciples are still puzzled and afraid. Diagnosing their mood, Jesus gathers up their questions in review and comment, which promise precisely the four prime necessities that the immediate future will demand.

1. The first and imperative need would be to conserve the immediate past. A vivid remembrance of him, of his words and deeds, of the inspiration of his presence would be essential if their rich experience in his company was not to be dissipated in mere forgetfulness. They had been slow to learn; that did not guarantee they would not be quick to forget.

As we have seen, both the Gospels and the Lord's supper

help to meet that need, but John's emphasis falls upon Christ's promise of the Spirit, Charles Wesley's "Remembrancer divine."

> These things I have spoken to you, while I am still with you. But the Counselor, the Holy Spirit, whom the Father will send in my name, he will teach you all things, and bring to your remembrance all that I have said to you.

This is a main theme upon which the upper room discourse, as now recorded, returns more than once. Here we note only the provision for immediate need. The Spirit will enable the disciples to recall, and increasingly to understand, all that Christ has given them.

Memory, after all, is more than the ability simply to recapture words and events. Memory sees experiences in context, interprets from the long view, evaluates, and garners meaning from what is recollected. No literature better illustrates the enrichment conferred upon experience by an interpretative memory than the Gospel of John itself.

But John is sure that more than memory is at work. The Spirit of Jesus himself, as he will say later, takes of the things of Christ and "shows" them to succeeding generations. Thus the first fear of the immediate future will be met for the Eleven — the fear of impoverishment through the departure of Christ, the fear of losing what they had so slowly gained, the fear of forgetting what it was imperative should never be forgotten. In all the confusions and new questions of the uncertain future, the Spirit would bring to mind all they would need to know.

2. If forgetfulness could impoverish, fear — and the fear of being afraid — could enervate and paralyze. There was no doubt of the peril ahead: to that second immediate need was addressed the repeated promise of sustaining peace:

> Peace I leave with you; my peace I give to you; not as the world gives do I give to you. Let not your hearts be troubled, neither let them be afraid.

"Peace," here, obviously has to be carefully understood. The one thing Jesus could not promise his men at that moment was "a quiet life" — nor yet a mind and heart untroubled by the pressures of the world. John has told us that the soul of Jesus had been thrice "troubled" (11:33; 12:27; 13:21), while ahead awaits the spiritual agony of Gethsemane. The promised "peace" is no selfish insulation, whether stoic or mystical, untouched by pain.

Given the full weight of the occasion and the imminent passion, the phrase "*my* peace" defines Jesus' meaning perfectly. What we see in him at that moment and throughout is a full awareness of suffering and conflict, of rejection and betrayal, combined with unswerving purpose, undeterred courage, and unhesitating faith. He shows no hint of distress or of panic, only of sad but unchanged dedication.

The peace Jesus promises was described by Frances Ridley Havergal:

> They say there is a hollow, safe and still,
>   A point of coolness and repose
> Within the centre of a flame, where life might dwell
> Unharmed and unconsumed . . .
>   There is a point of rest
> At the great centre of the cyclone's force
>   A silence at its secret source —
> A little child might slumber undistressed . . .
>
> So in the centre of these thoughts of God,
> Cyclones of power, consuming glory-fire,
> There, *there* we find a point of perfect rest
>   And glorious safety. . . .
> (Frances Ridley Havergal [1836–1879], "In the Hands of God")

But the fire and the cyclone are sometimes more earthly, heart-shaking, and painful than those Miss Havergal had in mind. It is just that inner poise amid a thousand shocks and swirling winds that Jesus knew, and promised to his disciples. "With Christ in the vessel we smile at the storm," said John Newton; but the tempest still rages.

This is the quality that we see in the martyr church, the peace that the world cannot give or understand. The ancient world had its stoics, pretending not to feel suffering; it had its masochists, delighting in pain: what it could not understand was Christian resilience, the inner resolve that acknowledged every fear, every agony, yet would not be deterred.

Such serene invincibility was not natural to the ordinary, unheroic men and women Jesus called into discipleship; it was a gift, a "legacy" they received from him. Yet, as a quality of character, it could not be imparted or injected from without; it had to be accepted and assimilated by self-discipline and self-command: "*Let not* your hearts be troubled," Jesus repeats his charge, "neither *let* them be afraid." Not even Jesus could rest their hearts upon his peace; they must do that themselves.

Such a promise of resilient inner peace was entirely appropriate to the immediate future. A sheltered, safe, unruffled serenity was not possible to Christians in Caesar's world; but a sustaining settlement of mind and the power to see things through — *that* they needed, and would find within their reach, if they took themselves in hand.

3. As the Spirit would conserve the past, and "peace" fortify them for the present, so the urgent question concerning the future is met by the promise of Christ's return.

> You heard me say to you, "I go away, and I will come to you." If you loved me, you would have rejoiced, because I go to the Father; for the Father is greater than I.

This, too, is a theme to which the discourse will return, but already the assurance should lift up their hearts and change their mood. The "I will come to you" is as clear and as certain as the "I go away"; yet the latter statement has overshadowed their evening and shocked their hopes, while the promise of return has stirred no excitement, brought them no consolation so far. But they should "have rejoiced."

Could they not see beyond their immediate sorrow and fear? His promised return should have changed despair to expectancy. His "going" was in truth no final rejection, certainly no defeat, no end to the great divine enterprise on which the Father had sent him. He was going "to the Father," and "the Father is greater than I." They should see his departure as the culmination of his mission, a kind of promotion, a homegoing and reward, and so the prelude to a glorious return.

So understanding it, they would have rejoiced for his sake. Instead, they had been absorbed in the consequences for themselves. Had they truly, passionately *loved* him, they would have been overjoyed at his prospect of glory — the rebuke here seems gentle, almost teasing, weaning them away from their fear for themselves to their hopes for him. For the ultimate outcome was assured: they would live to see that Calvary was no tragedy, but

77

indeed Christ's path to glory. And in glory he would return. That hope would sustain them in the darkest days.

4. Such provision for the immediate future is surely sufficient. Yet the nervous heart *will* ask upon what foundation such assurances were built. Was Jesus at that moment in any position to promise anything? Had not earlier promises of the great blessings of life within the kingdom proved elusive, as the crowds had turned away? Well-intentioned promises could come to nothing if the Master perished at the hands of evil men.

With perfect insight, Jesus insists that *already* he is in control of events and of eventualities:

> And now I have told you before it takes place, so that when it does take place you may believe. I will no longer talk much with you, for the ruler of this world is coming. *He has no power over me*; but I do as the Father has commanded me, so that the world may know that I love the Father. Rise, let us go hence.

"I have told you before. ... I will. ... I do. ... I love. ... Rise ...": the initiative remains with Jesus, not with the Jews, or Judas, or Caiaphas, or Pilate, or Caesar. Nor with "the ruler of this world" — "he has no power over me," a marvelous claim to make at that moment.

Men imagine they decide, think that they betray, frame the charge, pass their verdict, shape the cross, drive the nails; yet all the while it is Christ himself, in loving obedience to an accepted commandment of the Father, who takes the decisive action. His love for God and men brings him, and binds him, to the cross more firmly than all their plots and manacles. The circumstances are demonically engineered and humanly contrived: the consecration to God's will and to man's redemption that necessitates his death is his alone.

> Rebellious fool, what hast thy folly done?
> Controlled thy God, and crucified his Son?
> How sweetly has the Lord of life deceived thee!
> Thou shedd'st his blood, and that shed blood has saved
>   thee!

> (Francis Quarles [1592–1644], "Epigrams" [III.2])

So Jesus is already in command of all that is going forward, and can with confidence both predict and provide for the future. "Arise, let us go hence!" It is Christ's movement that is on foot, his moment has come. Nothing has gone wrong, nor will do so. The Eleven, and John's contemporaries in the Roman world, and we ourselves, may face tomorrow with equanimity. Nothing is left behind: we remember and share; the Spirit is here; our hearts are fortified with peace; the Lord will come — "Arise . . .!"

Grant unto us, O Lord, the royalty of inward happiness and the serenity that comes from living close to thee. Daily renew in us the sense of joy, and let Thine eternal Spirit dwell in our souls and bodies, filling every corner of our hearts with light and gladness; so that, bearing about with us the infection of a good courage, we may meet all that comes, of good or ill . . . with gallant and high-hearted happiness; giving Thee thanks always for all things.

*Illuminating
Discourse*

11:
The Commissioning:
God's Vine

JOHN 15:1-16

"I am the true vine, and my Father is the vinedresser. Every branch of mine that bears no fruit, he takes away, and every branch that does bear fruit he prunes, that it may bear more fruit. You are already made clean by the word which I have spoken to you. Abide in me, and I in you. As the branch cannot bear fruit by itself, unless it abides in the vine, neither can you, unless you abide in me. I am the vine, you are the branches. He who abides in me, and I in him, he it is that bears much fruit, for apart from me you can do nothing. If a man does not abide in me, he is cast forth as a branch and withers; and the branches are gathered, thrown into the fire and burned. If you abide in me, and my words abide in you, ask whatever you will, and it shall be done for you. By this my Father is glorified, that you bear much fruit, and so prove to be my disciples. As the Father has loved me, so have I loved you; abide in my love. If you keep my commandments, you will abide in my love, just as I have kept my Father's commandments and abide in his love. These things I have spoken to you, that my joy may be in you, and that your joy may be full.

"This is my commandment, that you love one another as I have loved you. Greater love has no man than this, that a man lay down his life for his friends. You are my friends if you do what I command you. No longer do I call you servants, for the servant does not know what his master is doing; but I have called you friends, for all that I have heard from my Father I have made known to you. You did not choose me, but I chose you and appointed you that you should go and bear fruit and that your fruit should abide; so that whatever you ask the Father in my name, he may give it to you."

HOWEVER we explain the abrupt movement from chapter 14 to chapter 15 (already noted), one point is beyond reasonable doubt: the earlier words "You are clean, but not all of you. . . . He knew who was to betray him" are linked directly with "every branch that bears fruit he *cleanses* that it may bear more fruit. . . . You are *made clean* by the word which I have spoken to you." The connection is obscured merely by the double meaning of a Greek word. The whole discussion about abiding in Christ (mentioned ten times) is Jesus' deliberate comment, uttered as soon as the interrupting questions have ceased, upon the disciple who did not "abide" and has now departed.

Reassurance was necessary, but the disciples had not been called out from the world simply for their own protection; one sure antidote to their fears was active work. That hostile world of which they were so afraid was to be their sphere of operations, and their target. *It is God's vineyard.* So when Jesus has answered their urgent questions, he returns (so to speak) to his own theme of chapter 13, the lessons to be drawn from the defection of Judas. One was that his hour had struck; the second, the need for mutual loyalty, repeated now in verse 12. Now a third vital lesson is drawn, the need to adhere closely to himself if the purpose of God is to be fulfilled and the whole mission of Jesus is to bear fruit.

The True Vine

The evocative metaphor Jesus now chooses had a very long history, and it filled his thought during this final week of his ministry. The great Isaiah had rebuked his own generation with a parable depicting Israel's profitless story. God had with infinite labor prepared a vineyard, and there had planted a choice vine, tending it and protecting it with great care — but it brought forth only wild, sour grapes.

Jewish piety had largely ignored the rebuke, but had accepted gladly the implication that Israel was "the planting of the Lord," a vine specially chosen and divinely tended in the earth to bring forth fruit for God among the nations. They inscribed the vine leaf on their native coinage, and a great golden vine sprawled across the massive door of the temple. Jews liked being the vine of God: the metaphor enshrined their deepest self-identity, feeding at once their piety and their patriotism (Ps. 80:8f.).

But Jesus told a parable of a fruitless tree. He left another tree also fruitless, withered at his word, shriveling outside the city gates as a powerful symbol of his judgment that the nation was even yet unprofitable to God. Still more daringly, within sight of that golden vine, in the very courtyard of the temple, Jesus told Isaiah's parable again. But this time, the "tenants" of the divine vineyard deliberately withheld the fruit from the vineyard's owner, and beat the servants he sent to collect it. When he resolved to overawe them by sending his son, his heir, the tenants decided to murder him, and take possession themselves. The owner's vengeance was swift: the vineyard would be given to others.

According to Luke, the listening crowd at this point broke in with shocked cries of "God forbid!" Mark adds that the authorities "tried to arrest him . . . for they perceived that he had told the parable against them. . . ." His version of the sacred metaphor had helped to seal his fate.

The thought of God's vine planting *may* have been in Jesus' mind also in the upper room, as he took a cup, gave thanks, and passed it around the table, saying, "Take this and divide it among yourselves, for I will drink no more of the fruit of the vine until that day I shall drink it new, with you, in my Father's kingdom." That seems a more distant echo of the same historic figure of speech, and it seems strange that John, who in chapter 6 speaks movingly about eating Christ's flesh and drinking his blood, neither records the founding of the supper nor recalls this saying that links the supper with the vine.

For all that, John does carefully preserve for us this "parable," or more strictly, this metaphor, spoken across the table, of the vine God has now planted in the earth. Here Jesus' comment is carried further: Not only is the divine vineyard taken from its ancient tenants and given to others; the vine itself is no longer the chosen nation, Israel, but Christ and all who, as branches, abide in him to bear fruit unto God. "I am the *true* vine . . . you are the branches" (vv. 1, 5).

It may well be that in a church tending to make too much of sacramental ceremony, John preferred to emphasize that abiding in the true and living vine was at least as important as drinking of the fruit of the vine in memory of a "bygone" Christ. If the poured wine speaks perpetually of his life once given for us, the flourishing vine speaks of his life ever renewed in us, flowing outward into visible fruitfulness.

Yet further provision is thus made for the years when "they will see him no more" and when a frightening world will daunt their spirits; *the church will be there*. John does not use that word, but he implies all that it means, just as he implies, in his indirect way, much about baptism (ch. 3), the Lord's supper (ch. 6), and the pastoral office (chs. 10, 20, 21). John describes, more clearly than do Mark or Luke, and almost as fully as Matthew does, the situation, tasks, and resources of the believing fellowship in the years ahead. Here, it is the vine planted in the earth by the Father, "the vinedresser," and tended by him in the vineyard of history. It consists of Christ and those abiding in him as branches to bear fruit for God by drawing life from Christ.

The Eleven are such branches by Christ's deliberate appointment and commission: "I am the vine, you are the branches. . . . You did not choose me, but I chose you and appointed you that you should go and bear fruit and that your fruit should abide. . . ." Both emphases are significant. The Eleven might have supposed that all depended on their choice to follow Christ, but the basic choice had in fact been his, in calling them to discipleship at all. And God requires fruit of long-keeping quality. Judas' defection gives an edge to the phrase "fruit that shall last," but sad experience by John's time of short-lived Christian profession may add weight to it. The nature of the "fruit" is not specified. In Isaiah 5 it included just and disciplined national life; here it clearly implies all that God has a right to expect from his people.

Jesus will say more presently about the task of the church and its commissioned leaders; here all is concentrated upon the appointment to bear fruit, and the imperative need to "abide" in the vine to that end.

The Missing Branch

The contrast with Judas, the branch that failed to abide in the vine, is obvious: the empty place at the table adds great force to Jesus' words. The vine needed "cleansing" (i.e., pruning), and it had been done; now Jesus comments on this with an analysis of spiritual declension that traces Judas' gradual decline.

For the open breach with Jesus was certainly not the beginning, but the end. Before that, there had been a failure to abide, an inward breaking away, then a visible withering. Only then followed the divine pruning and the gathering of the shriveled branch "to be burned." That awful climax would gain added meaning from Ezekiel's scathing description of vine wood as useful for nothing — neither to make utensils, nor to shape a peg to hang vessels upon, but only as fuel. The only value in a vine branch is to bear fruit or to be burned. And so it is, says Jesus, with disciples!

What to the Eleven, and to Judas himself, might appear a human decision, a resolve to "resign," to retire and give up, was in fact an act of God. "My Father is the vinedresser. . . . *He* prunes [it]." The first, hidden, inner separation of Judas from Jesus, the failure of understanding, the dwindling of sympathy, the rise of a critical spirit, led inevitably to the slight breaking-away in heart, seen in his change of mood and manner (the "withering" at the leaf-tips when the branch cracks from the main stem).

Later came the overt, public disagreement and criticism in the house at Bethany; and then the deliberate conspiracy to betray. But it was a word from Jesus, a final judgmental act of God, which finally separated Judas from the vine and sent him stealthily through the streets, ultimately to destroy himself. Judas is purged from the vine as a result of his own decisions, but the hand that bears the knife is "my Father's."

For Christians of all generations, there is no more searching passage in the whole of Scripture. Fail to abide, fail to draw inward life from the living Christ, and though for a while the outward life-style appears Christian, the leaves remain green and the branch tender, yet fruit fails, the visible breaking follows — with many plausible excuses — and we are removed, as even onlookers can see: "*they* gather them . . ." (literal translation). A favorite passage with many Christians, the parable of the true vine nevertheless carries a most somber warning.

Fortunately, what is meant by "abiding in the vine" is spelled out very clearly. Fruitfulness in Christ's service is assisted by personal gifts and training, but does not depend upon either. Fruit is always the overflow of a well-replenished life, and that calls for "abiding" in Christ's words, keeping in touch with him, and persisting in his love and in his joy.

To "have Christ's words abide in us" (v. 7) can only mean to nourish our minds upon his story and his message. To "keep his commandments" (v. 10) is to stay loyal at all times to his will for us. To "ask whatever we will" (v. 7) implies keeping in touch with him about our fruit bearing, and since such prayer is to arise from our union with him, there is no doubt that "it shall be done."

To "abide in his love" (v. 10), like "keeping ourselves in the love of God" (Jude 21), means being careful not to stray, in thought or action, to some far country of the soul where the love of God in Christ can no longer *reach* us — though as Jesus' parable shows, the love remains unchanged, and only our willfully "distancing ourselves" from God can keep it out.

To have Christ's joy in us, and at the full (v. 11), needs no explanation, though to speak of joy at that moment is astonishing. Such joy among Christian workers is rarer than it ought to be. Lucy Menzies, speaking of the great saints' ability to see the best side of all circumstances, adds, "This temper of the saints had also a little sparkle in it: a delicate humour was their crowning glory" ("Mirrors of the Holy," p. xi).

If there is no fruit without fullness, there is not likely to be any without winsomeness, too. To abide in Christ's teaching, obedience, fellowship, love, and joy is to live in him, abiding in the vine, and bearing fruit to God's everlasting glory.

> *That mystic word of Thine, O sovereign Lord*
> *Is all too pure, too high, too deep for me;*
> *Weary with striving, and with longing faint,*
> *I breathe it back again in prayer to Thee:*
> *Abide in me, I pray, and I in Thee . . .*
>
> *Abide in me; o'ershadow by Thy love*
> *Each half-formed purpose, and dark thought of sin:*
> *Quench, ere it rise, each selfish, low desire,*
> *And keep my soul as Thine, calm and divine.*
>
> *Abide in me; there have been moments blest*
> *When I have heard Thy voice and felt Thy power;*
> *Then evil lost its grasp, and passion, hushed,*
> *Owned the divine enchantment of the hour.*
>
> *These were but seasons, beautiful and rare:*
> *Abide in me, and they shall ever be;*
> *Fulfil at once Thy precept and my prayer —*
> *Come and abide in me, and I in Thee.*
>
> (Harriet Beecher Stowe [1812–1896], "That mystic word")

12:
"If the World Hates"

JOHN 15:9-16:4

*"As the Father has loved me, so have I loved you; abide in
my love. If you keep my commandments, you will abide in my
love, just as I have kept my Father's commandments and abide
in his love. These things I have spoken to you, that my joy may
be in you, and that your joy may be full.*

*"This is my commandment, that you love one another as I
have loved you. Greater love has no man than this, that a man
lay down his life for his friends. You are my friends if you do
what I command you. No longer do I call you servants, for the
servant does not know what his master is doing; but I have
called you friends, for all that I have heard from my Father I
have made known to you. You did not choose me, but I chose
you and appointed you that you should go and bear fruit and
that your fruit should abide; so that whatever you ask the Father
in my name, he may give it to you. This I command you, to love
one another.*

*"If the world hates you, know that it has hated me before
it hated you. If you were of the world, the world would love its
own; but because you are not of the world, but I chose you out
of the world, therefore the world hates you. Remember the word
that I said to you, 'A servant is not greater than his master.' If
they persecuted me, they will persecute you; if they kept my
word, they will keep yours also. But all this they will do to you
on my account, because they do not know him who sent me. If
I had not come and spoken to them, they would not have sin;
but now they have no excuse for their sin. He who hates me
hates my Father also. If I had not done among them the works
which no one else did, they would not have sin; but now they
have seen and hated both me and my Father. It is to fulfil the
word that is written in their law, 'They hated me without a
cause.' But when the Counselor comes, whom I shall send to
you from the Father, even the Spirit of truth, who proceeds from
the Father, he will bear witness to me; and you also are witnesses, because you have been with me from the beginning.*

"I have said all this to you to keep you from falling away. They will put you out of the synagogues; indeed, the hour is coming when whoever kills you will think he is offering service to God. And they will do this because they have not known the Father, nor me. But I have said these things to you, that when their hour comes you may remember that I told you of them."

THE besetting weakness of modern Christianity is sentimentality. That is, the naive belief that all people, given a fair chance, would be saints; the pathetic illusion that in God's world good will triumph without struggle, without cost; the unrealistic persuasion that order, protection, and reform may be achieved without resort to force; the foolish assumption that all points of view will be found to have truth in them, given sufficient "understanding."

Strangely, this tendency to self-deception is frequently miscalled "faith," and the underlying sentiment, that all is in reality well with the world but for some superficial and temporary indisposition, is supposed to be "basic Christianity." Christian thinkers of great influence have indeed striven to show that evil is unreal, a mere absence of good.

How anyone can reconcile such dangerous fantasies with the stark realism of Jesus passes comprehension. His words and warnings are often almost ruthless — "better not born," "better a millstone about his neck and drowned" are his verdicts on certain people; a rogues' gallery of acutely observed and bluntly described men of violence, revenge, avarice, heartlessness, folly, and deceit fills his parables. His call to discipleship at once warns that a cross may be the reward, with no privileged protection from the wild winds that blow or the floods that rise. And when he commissions his men for future tasks, he paints no rosy dream of fame and adulation, with a grateful world applauding. In fifteen verses, *hatred* and its characteristic manifestations in persecution, ignorance, murder, and revenge are mentioned fourteen times.

Hatred, Seen as Hatred

The reality and depth of the world's opposition to his mission preoccupied the Master's mind at this moment. He names its varied and resourceful forms: persecution such as he had endured in criticism and slander, attempts to entrap him by treacherous questioning, accusations of conspiracy with the devil and of madness; and such as he yet would undergo—betrayal, false accusation, trial, scourging, mockery, and death. Total rejection of their message would face the Eleven as it faced him. Banishment from the synagogues implied at once religious deprivation, social disgrace, and (in the popular mind) abandonment to the powers of evil.

The "killing" foreseen may imply (among Jews) the prescribed penalty for blasphemy or (among pagans) the fairly common lynching meted out to those who by reputed "atheism" (neglect of the local gods) bring disaster on the community. Some tincture of hindsight may here again lend color to John's record of Christ's words, but that Jesus often warned of the resourcefulness of the world's hatred is beyond doubt.

Among immediate occasions of such ill-treatment Jesus names alienation from the world's thought and ways. Evil men resent the "difference" of the good: "if you were of the world, the world would love its own; but because you are not of the world, but I chose you out of the world, therefore the world hates you." Say the wicked:

> Let us lie in wait for the righteous, because . . . he is clean contrary to our doings, he upbraideth us with our offending the law, and objecteth to our infamy. . . . He professeth to have the knowledge of God, and he calleth himself the child of the Lord. He was made to reprove our thoughts. He is grievous unto us even to behold: for his life is not like other men's, his ways are of another fashion. . . . Let us examine him with despitefulness and torture, that we may know his meekness and prove his patience. Let us condemn him to a shameful death. . . .

So the Wisdom of Solomon (2:12–20), a little before Jesus' day; but the experience of Noah and of Lot and of every pure and godly soul in every generation illustrates how the silent example of goodness and truth provokes of itself the envy, resentment, and malice of those who feel themselves rebuked.

Nevertheless, it is not the disciples' impulsive and imperfect goodness that will provoke the world's hostility, but their identification with Jesus:

. . . because I chose you out of the world. . . . Remember the word that I said to you, "A servant is not greater than his master." If they persecuted me, they will persecute you. . . . But all this they will do to you on my account. . . . If I had not come and spoken to them, they would not have sin; but now they have no excuse for their sin. . . . If I had not done among them the works which no one else did, they would not have sin; but now they have seen and hated both me and my Father.

Infrequently, and all too inadequately, Christians remind the world of him whose life, character, and message have become the standard of goodness and truth for succeeding generations — either the guiding conscience or the "bad conscience" of humankind. As the world knew not how to defend itself against Jesus except by destroying him, so it vents its hostility to all he stood for upon those whose witness keeps his memory alive.

If he had not come, or if having come he could be forgotten, men and women would have some excuse for the things they do: but he came, and the world is "without excuse" (as John says) for loving darkness instead of light. This is the true depth of evil — no mere want of education, "misunderstanding," "social deprivation," or immaturity, but willful hostility feeding upon culpable ignorance and so deepening ignorance further. "They do not know him who sent me. . . . They will do this because they have not known the Father, nor me." Why is this when he has come, and spoken, and done works that no one else did? Because "they have seen and hated both me and my Father. . . . They hated me without a cause. . . . He who hates me hates my Father also."

Seen? and yet hated thee? they did not see,
They saw thee not that saw and hated thee:
No, no, they saw thee not, O Life, O Love,
Who saw aught in thee that their hate could move.

Crashaw's protest is well meant, yet so it was, and among professedly "religious" people most of all. "The hour is coming when whoever kills you will think he is offering service to God":

I myself was convinced that I ought to do many things in opposing the name of Jesus of Nazareth. . . . I shut up many of the saints in prison. . . . when they were put to death I cast my vote against them. . . . tried to make them blaspheme. . . . in raging fury against them I persecuted them even to foreign cities.

So confesses one "educated according to the strict manner of the law of our fathers, being zealous for God," one who "according to the strictest party of our religion . . . always took pains to have a clear conscience toward God and toward men" (Acts 22:3; 26:9f.: 24:16). So self-deceiving can evil be, even in hearts conventionally, or traditionally, religious. "If the light that is in thee be darkness," said Jesus on another occasion, "how great is that darkness."

With what candor and realism Jesus pictures the future and takes the measure of the foe! Yet he is no pessimist. He forewarns not to discourage but to forearm against disillusionment: "I have said these things to you, that when their hour comes you may remember that I told you of them." And to evoke the reaction that the future will demand, that he will enable them to make.

Love — Expressed as Friendship

For hatred is by no means all that the coming years will know: the warnings of hatred are prefaced by nine references to *love*, the love in which their own experience is rooted, the love upon which their unity depends.

"As the Father has loved me"—what greater premise could be laid for any argument than that!—"As the Father has loved me, so have I loved you; abide in my love. . . . I have kept my Father's commandments and abide in his love. . . . This is my commandment, that you love one another as I have loved you." In that marvelous collocation of ideas an immeasurable relationship struggles for expression. The eternal unity of the Father and the Son, sustained unbroken on earth by the loving obedience of the Son-become-Servant, is now extended to embrace the Eleven in the Son's own love, and established as the—ideally unbreakable—unity of all who experience that love of God in Christ.

The only passage worthy to be set beside that for its sweeping grandeur of vision is an earlier statement in the same Gospel: "As the living Father sent me, and I live because of the Father, so he who eats me will live because of me" (6:57). There, *life* flows out of its eternal reservoir in God the Father, into this dying world in the person of Christ, the Son, who lives by the Father, and on through Christ into all who nourish their lives upon him. Here, *love*, anchored in the eternal relationship of Father and Son, is extended and expressed in the love the Son bears toward those who are his, and then further extended between those who owe everything to being so loved. Both life and love flow out of God through Christ into and between men: that is the gospel.

But the truth is not left in abstract terms. The love of Jesus for his men is about to be demonstrated in the most concrete and costly way imaginable. "Greater love has no man than this, that a man lay down his life for his friends." Thereafter the same love will be prolonged in an ever-deepening relationship of obedience and trust: "You are my friends if you do what I command you." That will be the disciples' situation henceforth, surrounded by the hatred of an unbelieving world but rooted in the friendship of Christ — and of fellow Christians. The world may hate, but they will abide in love, of Christ and of each other: neither friends of Jesus without each other, nor friends to each other except in and for him.

If the word "friend" seems inadequate for such a weight of meaning, let Jesus analyze it for us. First, we note that though the word Jesus used certainly means "friend," being used elsewhere of the friendship of neighbors, of Pilate and Herod, of Pilate and Caesar, of the "best man" for the bridegroom, yet "You are my friends" is literally "You are those I am loving" — holding in affection. Intimacy, loyalty, and trust are included in this friendship.

Secondly, so is unity of purpose: "You are my friends if you do what I command you." Jesus remains Lord; there is no diminution of authority in this friendship. But authority is balanced by understanding, as obedience is motivated by love. "No longer do I call you servants, for the servant *does not know* what his master is doing; but I have called you friends, for all that I have heard of my Father I have made known to you" — *all*, not his commands only, but also his intentions, his character, his love. Understanding prompts assent to what is enjoined; obedience so consenting is free, and springs from open, frank coincidence of will and unity of purpose. There is nothing servile about it: it is

Christian obedience. It is remarkable that in spite of this saying, so long preserved, apostolic Christians still preferred to call themselves "servants," and even "slaves," of Christ.

Thirdly, in battle or in civil strife, in persecution or in plague, true friendship could cost one's life. The risk of friendship is in view here. The words about laying down one's life for one's friends, coming as they do immediately after "love one another as I have loved you," obviously have a double reference: they illustrate his love, and set the standard for theirs. In coming years, the mutual loyalty Jesus commands will almost certainly involve risking life itself for the protection, concealment, and support of Christian brethren. Even as Jesus spoke, the peril awaiting them all in the quiet city threatened to test their loyalty, to him and to each other, before that night was through.

And fourthly, most friendships spring from the mutual attraction of like minds, drawn together by circumstance or shared need; but Jesus says, "You did not choose me, but I chose you, and appointed you that you should go and bear fruit . . ." — the word "you" each time being plural. This friendship was built upon his deliberate act and purpose, cemented by his clear command to remain united to him and to each other, and enriched by shared experience.

In the future, the experience of shared prayer will be especially important, replacing the present daily conversation with him, and giving a "vertical dimension" to their mutual friendship: "that what [all of] you ask the Father in my name, he may give it to you [all]." They must cherish with vigor and determination this "triangular" loyalty: not all the hatred the world can heap upon them must be allowed to break up their "friendship."

Finally, that friendship will be an integral part of that "witness" which they, along with the Spirit, will bear to the world. Witness seems a forlorn and weightless reply to hatred. By an almost invincible prejudice of thought we suppose resentment a more adequate reply to opposition than reasonableness, force more powerful than ideas, violence stronger than truth. Yet, as Paul reminds us, men "can do nothing against the truth": and witness is truth born of experience. It is the heart's own history, made eloquent by consistent living, made winsome by loving deed. The realism of the whole paragraph holds to its end; for there *is* no argument with which the world can contradict a sincere testimony confirmed by a fragrant life.

As each told repeatedly the story of his own soul's adventure with Christ, he would discover the power of truth spoken in love to silence opposition. As they stood loyally together in all peril, men and women would recognize that they were his disciples. And when in baffled fury the world resorted to violence, the blood of faithful martyrs would ever be found the living seed of a new generation of believers. As the classical historian T. R. Glover explained, the Christian faith survived first the onslaught of Rome and then her downfall because Christians "out-thought, out-lived, and out-died" their pagan contemporaries.

That was precisely the heroic witness for which in the upper room Jesus prepared his men, with no misleading forecasts and no false promises. But confirming, clarifying, and empowering their word would be the witness of the Spirit of God.

Do I truly and deeply believe that evil is real, positive, and powerful in the world, so that "if any one loves the world, love for the Father is not in him"? If that is true, it should be "blessed" to be reviled falsely, and persecuted; "dangerous" to have all men speak well of me. "Surely it is foolish to court the world's rejection, and frustrating, too, when I want to win the world . . . ?" Perhaps, yet when the chips are down —

Whoso has felt the Spirit of the Highest
Cannot confound nor doubt Him nor deny:
Yea with one voice, O world, tho' thou deniest,
Stand thou on that side, for on this am I.

(F. W. H. Myers [1843–1901], "Saint Paul")

13:
"Replacement" for Jesus

JOHN 14:15-18, 23-26; 16:4-15

"If you love me, you will keep my commandments. And I will pray the Father, and he will give you another Counselor, to be with you for ever, even the Spirit of truth, whom the world cannot receive, because it neither sees him nor knows him; you know him, for he dwells with you, and will be in you.

"I will not leave you desolate; I will come to you. . . ."

Jesus answered him, "If a man loves me, he will keep my word, and my Father will love him, and we will come to him and make our home with him. He who does not love me does not keep my words; and the word which you hear is not mine but the Father's who sent me.

"These things I have spoken to you, while I am still with you. But the Counselor, the Holy Spirit, whom the Father will send in my name, he will teach you all things, and bring to your remembrance all that I have said to you.

"I did not say these things to you from the beginning, because I was with you. But now I am going to him who sent me; yet none of you asks me, 'Where are you going?' But because I have said these things to you, sorrow has filled your hearts. Nevertheless I tell you the truth: it is to your advantage that I go away, for if I do not go away, the Counselor will not come to you; but if I go, I will send him to you. And when he comes, he will convince the world of sin and of righteousness and of judgment: of sin, because they do not believe in me; of righteousness, because I go to the Father, and you will see me no more; of judgment, because the ruler of this world is judged.

"I have yet many things to say to you, but you cannot bear them now. When the Spirit of truth comes, he will guide you into all the truth; for he will not speak on his own authority, but whatever he hears he will speak, and he will declare to you the things that are to come. He will glorify me, for he will take what is mine and declare it to you. All that the Father has is mine; therefore I said that he will take what is mine and declare it to you."

IN the whole of the upper room conversation, Christ's most surprising announcement, and his supreme promise for the dark days ahead, was his assurance that "another" would come to take his place and continue his ministry.

The Eleven had begun to grasp that Jesus really was "going away"; that he would "come again," and that their fellowship with him would be restored, was a natural hope. But that "another" could in any sense take his place with them was inconceivable. So were the hints Jesus had given about the manner of his return. The whole theme of his future "absent presence" was for them as difficult to grasp, and as unexpected, as it is for us.

As Jews, the Eleven were familiar with the name "Spirit" for the invisible divine power at work in nature, in artists, and in prophets, and with the promise that the Spirit would endow Messiah with every capacity for his work. Jesus had declared that the Spirit of the Lord was upon him, and had promised that, when hauled before governors and magistrates to answer for their faith, the disciples would find that the Spirit would inspire their answers, pleading their case as a divine "advocate."

By the time John wrote, much had happened to enlarge and enrich Christian understanding of the Spirit. Pentecost had come, and had continued, and the Spirit had conferred an altogether new level of experience, a totally new quality of character, and unprecedented equipment for service — miraculous "gifts" of speech, healing, leadership, and the like — upon the church. The experience had been analyzed memorably by Paul in Romans 8; the character had been described, also by Paul, in Galatians 5 and 1 Corinthians 13; the equipment had been illustrated dramatically by Luke in Acts, and by Paul in 1 Corinthians 12–14.

It is remarkable, therefore, that John's forecast of the functions of the Spirit owes nothing to that Pentecostal and Corinthian experience, that it does not mention "gifts," and that it is wholly independent of both Paul and Luke. One might almost imagine that he knew nothing of how the promise of the Spirit had been fulfilled in the sixty intervening years. Even the most familiar name, "Holy Spirit," occurs here only once (14:26), and then only as a second title to identify "the Counselor." Yet that name explicitly distinguishes "the Spirit" from the innumerable and ubiquitous *evil* spirits believed to work man's undoing.

John's emphasis in recording Jesus' words differs from the church's first thought about the Spirit in two vital respects.

The Form of the Contemporary Christ

One may trace in the New Testament a movement of thought concerning the Spirit from something "shed forth" or "poured out," an element one may be immersed ("baptized") in or with, and a power that "comes" or "falls" upon Christians to the fully personal view for which the Spirit "wills," "loves," "speaks," "calls," "prays," has a "mind," and "loves." And it continues on to the conception of "the Spirit of Jesus," "the Spirit of Christ," relating the Spirit and the risen Jesus so closely that Paul can say "the Lord is the Spirit."

John 13–17 completes this movement of thought. The coming Spirit is identified with the departing Christ as (so to speak) "another self" in whom Christ will continue to be present. This is stated explicitly, almost boldly, as an *advantage* to be gained by Christ's departure:

> Nevertheless I tell you the truth: it is to your advantage that I go away, for if I do not go away, the Counselor will not come to you; but if I go, I will send him to you.

That is an amazing verse. The fleshly presence of the visible, tangible Christ in the upper room among his men is to be exchanged for a presence transcending all human limitations, a *universalized* Christ. "Another" will be to the disciples all that Christ has been to them. He will not come until Christ has "left," but his coming makes Christ's going an advantage — apparent departure proving itself in experience to be only a more intimate approach.

This explains and elaborates the word already spoken of the Spirit (14:17): "you know him, for he dwells with you, and will be in you," Freed from the limits of time and space, the Christ of the coming years will, by the Spirit, be infinitely nearer to his own than he has been, no longer only "with" but "in" them. So understood, the Spirit does not supply the deficiency left by an absent Christ; he mediates, and conveys, Christ's nearer presence still. That is why Jesus does not leave them "bereaved" (14:18; literally "orphaned"), for he is not deserting them. He remains by, or "as," the Spirit. The personalizing of the Spirit of power of the Old Testament, and his identification as the Spirit of Christ, are here alike finalized.

For all that, there is some sense in which the disciples' situation will be changed. The Spirit is "another" advocate (14:16), the same yet not the same; Christ will "go away," even though he sends the Spirit to remain with them "for ever." The physical presence so dear to the Eleven will be lost, and they must face that loss. The resurrection stories relate that for forty days the disciples adjust to a presence sometimes seen and touched, sometimes unseen and intangible, coming unheralded and "vanishing out of their sight." Gradually, the sense of his constant nearness, whether seen or unseen, fills their days.

Then his visible, tangible appearances ceased, so that his spiritual, universal, and timeless presence might replace them. The Servant-Christ of the earthly ministry became the risen Christ of the church's postascension experience, and of our own time. This is the massive step forward that the Christian gospel takes in man's awareness of God, from the sense of inherent mystery, awe, and often dread to God seen, trusted, and loved in Jesus and intimately known, depended upon, and yielded to, in confidence and great joy, as indwelling Spirit.

The Spirit is indeed the form of the contemporary Christ in each succeeding generation. "I will come to you. . . . I in you" (14:18, 20). That stupendous promise is sufficient for the tasks and problems of every age — as Jesus now shows.

The Ministries of the Spirit

Almost as far-reaching is John's change of emphasis in recording the promised functions of the Spirit in the interadvent years, as not the Spirit of *power* bestowing "gifts" and capacities for service, but the Spirit of *truth* revealing Christ more perfectly to the ongoing church. This ministry in the realm of truth is expounded in the upper room discourse with exceptional fullness.*

1. *Comforter — Counselor.* The root idea here is anyone — friend, neighbor, family member, priest, or professional advocate (British, Queen's Counsel; American, Counselor) — who in an

---

* Inevitably, the exposition here overlaps a little the treatment of the same verses in *The Answer is the Spirit* (Philadelphia: Westminster Press, and Edinburgh: St. Andrew Press).

emergency is "called alongside to help" in whatever way the need requires.

From this root idea spring several shades of meaning. The friend who hurries to one's side in trouble "comforts" in a general way, though sympathy, pity, and the emotional sharing of pain was not the intended meaning when KJV/AV chose the title "Comforter" for the Spirit. "Comforter" belonged with "fort," "fortification," "fortitude," and meant one who fortifies greatly, who imparts courage — in modern terms, an enabler of others.

Legally, the one who stands beside the accused to answer on his behalf is called Advocate, or Counsel. This title faintly echoes Jesus' promise that the Spirit will give to the persecuted the words to answer to governors and kings. Perhaps more faintly still, the title recalls the "accuser of our brethren" who in the courts of heaven plays "devil's advocate" *against* the godly (Job 1:6–12 where "the satan" means "the adversary"; cf. Rev. 12:10). In Romans 8:27, the Spirit makes intercession for the saints; in 1 John 2:1 Jesus Christ the righteous is the "advocate" for sinful people.

Pastorally, however, the title has a third dimension, for in Greek "counselor" (or "paraclete") is related to exhortation, counseling, encouragement ("paraclesis"); the ministry toward one's fellow Christians that aims to uphold, to edify, to encourage. This is the main purpose of in-church preaching in the New Testament. Barnabas, being "full of the Holy Spirit," was for this reason nicknamed "son of encouragement," as one who ever came alongside weaker souls to uplift and strengthen (Acts 15:37–39; 9:26f.). So gracious a gift for "strengthening one's brethren" and bringing the best out of others was very early recognized as a clear mark of those in whom "the Comforter" had his way. This was his work.

2. *Spirit of truth*. Jesus has many things to say, the disciples many things to learn: the answer to this need is the promise of the Spirit who (as we have seen) will bring all things they have heard and seen back to their remembrance, illuminating their hindsight, guiding them in "all the truth." Each detail of this teaching ministry of the Spirit is of central importance still, as he "replaces" Jesus as teacher, bringing to Christian minds truth still to be understood, and making all timelessly relevant.

The Spirit's *subject* is Christ. "He will not speak on his own authority, but whatever he is given to speak, that he will say. . . . He will glorify me, for he will take what is mine and declare it to you." That implies no limitation of the Spirit's ministry, since Jesus can say, *"All that the Father has* is mine; therefore I said that he will take what is mine and declare it to you." But it does provide a well-founded test of what is, or is not, "of the Spirit." The one sure mark of the Spirit's ministry is that he will not speak about himself. What is truly of the Spirit will be recognizably Christ-centered, never Spirit-centered. Jesus said so.

The special *manner* of the Spirit's teaching ministry is suggested by the words "he will guide you into all the truth." That scarcely indicates the imparting of new information about Jesus: we have that information in the Gospels. Nor does "guiding into" truth promise supernatural revelation through visions and voices. What is foreseen here is progressive discovery, through experience and practice equally with reflection, of the full implications and the continually new applications of what they have already learned through Christ.

Thus the Spirit of truth is the spur and guide of all Christian development in every generation, the Spirit of intellectual and moral *progress*.

3. *Convictor of the world*. As Spirit of truth also *to the world*, the Spirit of Jesus will prosecute the world with the same power of argument with which he defends Christians. For he will continually keep before the world's conscience the truth concerning Jesus.

He will convict the world of sin for rejecting Christ. That is the chief sin, in John's eyes: that Jesus should come to his own home and his own people receive him not; that light should come into the world, and men love darkness rather than light. This is the judgment: since by belief in Christ people have life, to disbelieve or to reject him is to "abide in death." Of that supreme folly, the ultimate sin, the Spirit will convince men and women.

He will convince the world of righteousness by showing how Jesus was vindicated, proved to have been right, by his resurrection and ascension. And he will convince men and women of judgment, by showing them that "the ruler of this world" is judged, the power of evil is broken, and its hold over them is relaxed, since Jesus died (cf. 16:11 and 12:31).

Just how the Spirit will accomplish all this is not explained. Certainly he will not indwell the world, which cannot receive, see, or know him (14:17). John knew, by the time he wrote, that the Spirit would work upon men and women through the Spirit-filled church. It would scarcely be true to say, in that upper room, to men so fearful and unready, that the church would convince the world! But the Spirit, through the church, adding authority and power to their witness and manifesting in the lives of believers the truth and power of Christ, would — and did — and does — convince men and women of the real nature and cost of sin, of the meaning of righteousness as seen in Jesus, and of the judgment wrought upon evil through the cross of Christ.

4. *Spirit of prophecy*. This means not merely "of prediction," but in the fuller Old Testament sense of illuminating events and problems as they arise, irradiating the way forward, foreshadowing the outcome of actions and attitudes: so "he will declare to you the things that are to come."

The future (as Jesus always insists) is "in the Father's own authority" (Acts 1:7), and it is not for us to know the times or the seasons, or the things God has prepared for those who love him (1 Cor. 2:9), until the Spirit makes them plain. As the future unfolds, the Spirit will show as much as we need to know, guiding our feet and assuring our hearts that all that God has planned is coming to pass.

Once again we must bear in mind the double timing in the record. When Jesus spoke, "the things" immediately "to come" were his own death and resurrection, about which the disciples would sorely need the Spirit's illumination if their faith was to survive. But when John wrote, "the things to come" carried for him and his fellow believers another meaning, signifying all the way into the dark future, the outcome of the church's struggle with Rome, and "the last things." This, too, the Spirit would illumine, leading always forward into God's tomorrow, on to the end of time.

In such a description of the Spirit's function in the church, the earlier, more bizarre manifestations, the "extraordinary miracles" (to borrow Luke's phrase, Acts 19:11), have fallen into the background, and a more "intellectual" ministry has come to be valued amid the new problems, the philosophic challenges, and the confusions and denials of the wider world at the end of the century. As a complement to the commissioning of his men, and his assurance of divine friendship amid the world's hatred, Christ's promise of the inspiring, ennabling, cooperating Spirit was wholly relevant and bracing.

Probably at that moment the Eleven might still question the word "It is to your advantage that I go away," just as, in our hearts, each of us still wishes we might have seen the Lord, and might carry the memory of his physical presence. Perhaps that is because we have still not grasped the wonder of the promise, "I will come to you. . . . I will not leave you orphaned. . . . The Comforter, the Spirit of truth, dwells with you and will be in you."

To paraphrase words of a great European scholar, God has never drawn a line under the apostolic age and said "That's that!"

I dared not hope that Thou wouldst deign to come
And make this lowly heart of mine Thy home,
That Thou wouldst deign, O King of kings, to be
E'en for one hour a sojourner in me;
Yet art Thou always here, to help and bless,
And lift the load of my great sinfulness.

(E. Hatch [1835–1889])

14:
The Ultimate Future

JOHN 16:16–28

*"A little while, and you will see me no more; again a little
while, and you will see me." Some of his disciples said to one
another, "What is this that he says to us, 'A little while, and you
will not see me, and again a little while, and you will see me';
and, 'because I go to the Father'?" They said, "What does he
mean by 'a little while'? We do not know what he means." Jesus
knew that they wanted to ask him; so he said to them, "Is this
what you are asking yourselves, what I meant by saying, 'A little
while, and you will not see me, and again a little while, and you
will see me'? Truly, truly, I say to you, you will weep and lament,
but the world will rejoice; you will be sorrowful, but your sorrow
will turn into joy. When a woman is in travail she has sorrow,
because her hour has come; but when she is delivered of the
child, she no longer remembers the anguish, for joy that a child
is born into the world. So you have sorrow now, but I will see
you again and your hearts will rejoice, and no one will take your
joy from you. In that day you will ask me no questions. Truly,
truly, I say to you, if you ask anything of the Father, he will give
it to you in my name. Hitherto you have asked nothing in my
name; ask, and you will receive, that your joy may be full.*

*"I have said this to you in figures; the hour is coming when
I shall no longer speak to you in figures but tell you plainly of
the Father. In that day you will ask in my name; and I do not
say to you that I shall pray the Father for you; for the Father
himself loves you, because you have loved me and have believed
that I came from the Father. I came from the Father and have
come into the world; again, I am leaving the world and going to
the Father."*

ANOTHER sudden babble of questions interrupts Jesus, and
with them we have to take account not simply of double timing
in the record but of triple timing. Words that Jesus spoke during

his own earthly time are recalled by John for the instruction of readers in *his* time, concerning a time still to come!

If we find that confusing, so did the disciples:

> Some of his disciples said to one another, "What is this that he says to us, 'A little while, and you will not see me, and again a little while, and you will see me'; and, 'because I go to the Father'?" They said, "What does he mean by 'a little while'? We do not know what he means."

Their bewilderment is well expressed in such repetitious questioning. But Jesus adds further to the repetition:

> Jesus knew that they wanted to ask him; so he said to them, "Is this what you are asking yourselves, what I meant by saying, 'A little while and you will not see me, and again a little while and you will see me'? . . ."

This is most uncharacteristic. John is not usually so tedious, and never clumsy.

One detail is clear. Spoken in the upper room on the night on which Jesus was betrayed, the words that provoked the questions, "A little while, and you will see me no more; again a little while, and you will see me," referred directly to Jesus' imminent death, burial, and resurrection. The first "little" while would be but a few hours; the second, just three days. There was nothing in this to bewilder the Eleven. That Jesus should die at all was certainly strange to them, though by the end of that evening it was surely becoming clear. The points that aroused questioning were the "little while you will see not . . . a little while you will see," and "because I go to the Father" — not simply the fact of his death.

But by the time John wrote, all perplexities about Christ's death, resurrection, and ascension had been gloriously clarified by Easter and its aftermath. In view of that, John's reiteration of the bewildering phrase "a little while" *seven times* could hardly be more intriguing. Why this repetition, long after the fears and puzzlement are past?

As if to alert attention still more, Jesus adds a metaphor about a woman's joy when after long travail her child is born. That figure is not elsewhere used of Jesus' passion and seems entirely inappropriate to Jesus' rising from the tomb. Nor does the further counsel about asking questions and about prayer seem very relevant to the approaching three days. In any case, what possible purpose for John's readers or for us would be served by recalling this whole incident?

That metaphor of travail provides the clue. The woman-in-travail figure had a long and apposite association with prophecies about *the last days*. It began in forecasts of "messianic woes" or travail expected to precede the messianic kingdom, a familiar theme in later Jewish apocalyptic and possibly reflected in the strange prophecy of Revelation 12. More important, the figure had already been used by Jesus in describing his own final advent (Mark 13:8, Greek), and Paul echoes that thought (1 Thess. 5:3). It is plain that by the time of John's writing, the language of verse 21 had clear overtones of advent, rather than of Easter.

At once we recall that all the Gospels record, during the last week of Jesus' ministry, a long discourse on the last things, though John (we said) tells nothing of bridesmaids, talents, fig trees, or sheep and goats, and the fall of Jerusalem is left behind by some twenty-five years. Nevertheless, John too knows that part of the perplexity of that last week concerned how all was going to turn out — what would be the ultimate end of this great experience with Jesus and of the mission that underlay it?

Coping with Delay

John's parallel with the great prophetic chapters of Matthew, Mark, and Luke may seem slight, but he has lived to see disappointment and to think very deeply. John's hindsight, back across the vista of the years since Jesus "left," is even longer than Matthew's and Luke's. His advent hope has been toned down to black-and-white terms, without parables or drama — though the hope is still there.

So the intervening years, with their delay and perplexity, have given new meaning to that remembered questioning:

> What is this that he says to us, "A little while, and you will not see me, and again a little while and you will see me. . . ." *What does he mean by "a little while"*?

That was precisely the question that by John's time had troubled the church for a quarter of a century. Behind John's record of the upper room inquiries we can hear, if we listen, the puzzled muttering of the church in John's own time — "What did he mean by 'a little while'?"

Had not Jesus promised to return, and soon? Paul thought so, when he advised the Corinthians that there was no time for marrying; the Thessalonians thought so, when they worried about Christians who had died before Christ came again, and some gave up their daily employment to await the end. But the end had not come. The "little while" between seeing and seeing again had stretched already beyond all expectation, over three generations. All around John, Christian hearts were asking, "What did that 'little while' really mean?"

The church had wrestled with its disappointment manfully and ingeniously. One explanation was that with the Lord dates do not count: a thousand years are just one day (2 Pet. 3:8)! Some had persuaded the Thessalonians, and readers of the Pastoral Epistles, that Christ had already come (2 Thess. 2:1f.; 2 Tim. 2:18). Paul's reply to the problem was that a considerable program of prior events had first to be fulfilled (2 Thess. 2:3f.) — together with a sober readiness for the Lord's return at *any* time.

The Pastoral Epistles counsel preparation for the long haul through history by training the next generation for Christ's service (2 Tim. 2:2). Matthew insists again and again that "the end is not yet," and that only foolish bridesmaids are unprepared for a long wait, when "the Master delayeth his coming." All the offered "explanations" only illustrate the urgency of the questions.

John's Answer

John's reaction to the church's bewilderment over the delayed advent was to let us overhear the church's anxious questioning, and to offer to us two certainties and two promises. In this light, his record of similar questions asked in the upper room becomes urgently relevant to the original readers, and to ourselves, for whom the delayed advent remains a test of faith.

One certainty is that *Christ is here*. Much of the program for the future that Jesus outlined in the upper room had centered upon the coming of the Spirit, "Christ's other self," "the form of the contemporary Christ in succeeding generations." John and his contemporaries had seen this fulfilled in the throbbing life of the expanding, enduring, resilient church. One need then, as

now, in face of the delayed advent, was never to allow anticipation of Christ's coming to overshadow the truth, or diminish
the experience, of his constant "imminent" presence. "The Lord
is at hand" — at your elbow.

The other certainty, nevertheless, is that *Christ will come*.
John says nothing to cast doubt upon the return of Jesus in glory.
A resurrection at the last day figures four times in chapter 6;
"I will come again" in chapter 14 (vv. 3, 18); and "until I come"
in chapter 21; while 1 John 3 has "When he shall appear we
shall be like him." If "I go away" was true, so is "I will come
again." He is not defeated, but "going," and going "to the Father."
This night is not the end: that lies ahead. If the new age has
been inaugurated in the power of the Spirit, it has still to be
consummated in the appearing of the Christ.

Our other need, therefore, is never to allow the truth and
experience of the presence of the Spirit to obscure the promise
of the advent and the End. So much of modern Christianity has
no future dimension, no certain hope; and the church has never
been powerful when she did not know where she was going.

"A little while and you will see me"; the disciples repeat it,
Jesus says it again, and, with endearing change, yet once more:
"I will see you again. . . ." That seeing will bring joy, inalienable
and unending. At that time their whole situation will be re-
versed: now, the world rejoices while they are about to grieve;
then, they will rejoice and the world will be unable any longer
to plunder their joy.

They had joy, no doubt, at his resurrection, but imprison-
ment, flogging, and martyrdom have followed. For the moment
the perspective lengthens. John is evidently right to catch in the
words of Jesus the double application, and to urge his questioning readers at the end of the century to listen again, more carefully, to the reply Jesus gave to the Eleven. Certainly he will
come: but did he not also say there must first be a time of
absence, and of weeping?

Did he not warn that for a time they would *not* see him in
person or in power? As with a woman awaiting her child, the
time will drag, the travail increase — John's Gospel was pub-
lished, in all probability, on the eve of Domitian's persecution.
Deliverance and fulfillment will not be so soon as the Eleven —
and John's readers — had hoped. But *he will come* — though be-

tween the going and the coming stretches an interim of waiting, of witnessing, even of weeping, *as he said*.

Of the conditions of that interim little new is added here, and that little is somewhat obscure. It certainly does not apply to the hours between Jesus' death and resurrection. It seems probable (but not certain) that in the original, deliberate distinction is made between two forms of asking: asking questions, and asking for things. If that is true, then two promises appear to be appended to John's two certainties.

1. The interim will bring its own clarification. They will no longer assault Jesus with questions, as they had been doing that evening. The Spirit of truth will lead by experience into discovery, answering their questions as they arise. They will know all they need to know, no longer expressed in figures, parables, and metaphors but plainly, by the inner certainty of spiritual insight. Especially will they know "of the Father" (v. 20). In spite of the pressures and the perils, the waiting and the longing, they shall not miss their way, nor lose their faith. All will become clear.

2. On the other hand, the interim between the going and the coming will (Jesus repeats) be a time for keeping in touch by prayer that shall prevail. The earlier promise of successful prayer (15:16) is now strengthened: not Jesus' name and intercession only but the Father's own love for them guarantees the answer. From now on, prayer must be the means of communication on their side, as the Spirit's ministry will be on his side.

During the period of waiting and travail, the "little while" of disappointment, the lines of communication will remain open, fellowship will remain unbroken, and strength will remain sufficient for work and for endurance. Such are his promises for the interadvent years: neither illumination nor resources shall fail, until he come.

Of course John has not "explained" the delayed advent. He is not interested in theoretic questions. Disciples will be well informed and well equipped for what life will demand — that is sufficient. John has not "rationalized" the church's disappointment, nor has he claimed that all has been fulfilled in some unexpectedly "spiritual" fashion, though he has balanced advent excitement with the joy of the Spirit's presence, holding the tension of dual truths in a mature faith.

Nor, again, has John "demythologized" the language of the

advent hope in favor of some general spiritual truths about the ultimate survival of "spiritual values," though it is true he tells us nothing of the place, time, form, or accompanying "signs" of Jesus' return, details so beloved of apocalyptists. John has met head-on the questioning in earnest Christian hearts by recalling the similar questions asked of Jesus long ago. "Listen," John seems to say, "to how Jesus answered on the night of peril and foreboding. He promised not to leave us uncomforted, and he *has* given us his Spirit. He warned that a time of travail would ensue, relieved by illumination and by prayer — and so it has been. He promised he will come again in glory — and so he will." Meanwhile, we are already in touch with the coming Lord, whose absence proves to be only a nearer kind of presence, and whose presence is the guarantee of his yet more glorious appearing.

As the darkness deepened beyond the windows of the upper room; as Judas organized betrayal with priests and temple police, with arms and the prearranged sign of the kiss; as Caiaphas sent messengers to warn the Sanhedrin of an "emergency" meeting and planned the first informal interrogation in the house of Annas; as all the steps and preparations for his own destruction and for the disaster overhanging the nation moved now inevitably forward, Jesus looked ahead into the bleak, forbidding future. What did that future hold for these he loved?

> *The church would be there*, standing together in loyalty, witnessing, bearing fruit, doing greater things;
> *The Spirit would be there*, teaching, inspiring, leading forward, defending the disciples and convicting the world;
> *The advent hope would be there*, lifting their hearts again and again in dark days with an undying optimism and foretaste of glory.

By those three perpetual springs of spiritual renewal, Christians have lived and labored, endured and died, through twenty centuries.

> *What can we do, o'er whom the unbeholden*
> *Hangs, in a night with which we cannot cope?*
> *What, but look sunward, and with faces golden*
> *Speak to each other softly of a hope?*
>
> (F. W. H. Myers [1843–1901], "Saint Paul")

He is coming, like the glory of the morning on the wave;
He is wisdom to the mighty, He is succour to the brave;
So the world shall be his footstool.
and the soul of time his slave:
Our God is marching on.

(Julia Ward Howe [1819–1910], "Battle Hymn of the Republic")

15:
Magnificent Ending

JOHN 16:28–33

"I came from the Father and have come into the world; again, I am leaving the world and going to the Father."

His disciples said, "Ah, now you are speaking plainly, not in any figure! Now we know that you know all things, and need none to question you; by this we believe that you came from God." Jesus answered them, "Do you now believe? The hour is coming, indeed it has come, when you will be scattered, every man to his home, and will leave me alone; yet I am not alone, for the Father is with me. I have said this to you, that in me you may have peace. In the world you have tribulation; but be of good cheer, I have overcome the world."

WITH an almost audible sigh of relief the Eleven cease their questioning. "Ah, now you are speaking plainly, not in any figure!" The words that evoke that tribute are indeed plain: they form a perfect summary of the disciples' exact position, and an equally perfect summary of the truth about Jesus.

> . . .The Father himself loves you, because you have loved me and have believed that I came from the Father. I came from the Father and have come into the world; again I am leaving the world and going to the Father.

As the long evening of talk draws to a close, the simple statements put all that is essential into briefest compass and true perspective. "You have loved me": that pinpoints the personal emotional bond that holds them to him, the fundamental relationship upon which all will depend. "Lovest thou me?" he will ask later — no more than that, and no less.

"You have believed that I came from the Father": that focuses the fundamental response of faith, the intellectual basis, or content, of their love — conviction of his divine origin and mission. Endless arguments have unfolded the further implications of that conviction — but that is the spring from which all Christian theology flows.

"I came from the Father . . . into the world . . . leaving the world . . . going to the Father": Jesus adds very simply his own confirmation of their faith, and at the same time derives all from the ultimate source of everything Christian — the love of God for men and women. One senses too that in this eternal movement of Christ, coming from God into the world, leaving the world and going to the Father, the world's rejection of him is a mere incident, painful but in the long sweep of divine purpose unimportant; whereas their recognition and response, their faith and love, are all-important, are crucial for the future.

Their Confession of Faith

So much is clear, and moving; less clear are the words they add:

Now we know that you know all things, and need none to question you; by this we believe that you come from God.

We expect the remark to run "you know all things and need not to question anyone." But we recall that throughout, John has stressed that Jesus could read men's minds and hearts. His divine insight into Nathanael's meditation under the fig tree convinced Nathanael that Jesus was Son of God. The same insight into "what was in man" prevented his trusting himself to men (2:24f.). He knew from the first who did not believe on him, as he knew who was to betray him (6:64; 13:11). Throughout the evening Jesus had been answering questions put to him, not according to their words but according to the intention behind the words, and sometimes he had "divined" the questions they whispered to each other.

This faultless insight (they now appear to say) makes all questioning for him unnecessary; he understands already what they wish to know, and speaks to their unspoken need. Such divine understanding convinces them that Jesus came from God. We have seen that John wrote his Gospel to relate by what ways many came to faith, so that the readers might find faith for themselves (20:31); here, faith is insight answering to insight, truth "sparking" between sensitive and perceptive minds. There is perhaps no deeper definition of religious conviction.

Jesus' first response to this final confession of faith from his men before his passion is both serious and sad. He does indeed know them, more intimately than they realize, more than they know themselves. "Do you now believe?" The "now" may echo the reply earlier to Philip, "Have I been with you so long, and yet you do not know me . . . ?" implying, "Do you now *at last* believe?" More probably his "now" takes up their own words "Now we know . . ." but with a sad foresight that underlines the "now": it is easy to confess faith here, in the shelter and the fellowship of the upper room, but

> The hour is coming, indeed it has come, when you will be scattered, every man to his own home and will leave me alone. . . .

It will not be Judas only!

Among the four evangelists, only Luke omits that terrible warning on this last day of their earthly fellowship. Such was the inner depth of his pain, on that fateful night: divine insight is not all advantage when one's friends are frail! Nevertheless he believed in them, and entrusted his cause to them. "Having loved his own who were in the world, he loved them to the end." Strange to think that *his* faith in *us* is likewise important to God's plan — strange, and humbling.

His Confession of Faith

But the conversation is not permitted to end in sadness and warning. As a second response to their confession of faith, the courage and confidence of Jesus rise to a magnificent assertion of his own faith — the faith in which he dies — even as he brings that memorable evening to an end by rising to pray. He steps forth to the garden (18:1), and to all that lies beyond it, with three strong certainties upholding his heart.

1. "*I am not alone, for the Father is with me.*" His disciples will leave him, but the Father does not ("is" with me, not "will be"). John tells of no "cry of dereliction" uttered by the dying Jesus, "My God, my God, why hast thou forsaken me?" He insists on the complementary truth, expressed also in Jesus' final

prayer, "Father, into thy hands I commit my spirit," that Christ and the Father are one.

Yet once more we are reminded of the Servant's perfect unity of purpose with him who sent him. The subordination and dependence of the Servant-Son holds to the end: "I do as the Father has commanded me, so that the world may know that I love the Father" (14:31). But so does the other side of that perfect unity: the Father never forsakes the Son. Jesus is never alone.

That meant much to him, as the shadows darkened around him. It meant much also to the disciples, and means much to every Christian in years of trial. Christ's sublime sense of unity with God gains immeasurably in depth as he reaffirms it on this night above all nights, beneath that very cross which appears so violently to contradict it. Not only are we sure that Jesus' mission was divine; not only are we certain that he went forward firmly to his death with unshaken conviction that he was one with God in what he was doing and suffering; we know also that in the darkest, most tragic hour the presence of God did not fail him.

And that it will not fail us.

2. *"I have said this to you that in me you may have peace."* The note already struck twice (14:1, 27) sounds a third time, almost incongruously in these circumstances. "Peace" — *shalom* — is also "farewell!" His own inner assurance of the Father's unfailing presence only evoked a deeper compassion for their weakness, moved by his insight to understand both their panic at this moment, and their penitence for it. So once more he offers his peace.

Into that peace will enter all the reassurance he has uttered about the future, about the Father's love and the Spirit's presence, about his choice and commissioning of themselves: but most of all, it is *in him* they will have peace, as surely as *in the world* they will have tribulation. The world professes to long for peace, and continually destroys it. "In the world . . . tribulation" is a statement of fact, the testimony of experience: "in me peace," always, in every circumstance, in every sense, and forever, is a divine promise.

Here again (as in 14:27) Jesus does not guarantee peace "in the world." But Christians live in two environments simultaneously, in the physical and social context determined by their origins and circumstances, and "in Christ," a spiritual context of faith, ideals, and fellowship. "In me," Jesus promises, ". . . you may have peace" — whatever the circumstances, as the heart stays itself upon the steadfast purpose, high courage, and unwavering faith of Jesus. It was for this he was opening his heart to them (v. 33), that they might shelter within his faith and share his serenity.

Toward the end of the first century, John fully understood the value of this promise. It had been a stormy sixty years since that night in Jerusalem, years full of change and of much suffering, years marked by expansion of horizons, by unprecedented challenges to thought and to courage, and by many martyrdoms. Yet the church had shown a certainty, a clarity and conviction, a steadiness of character, that not all the might of Rome could quench. In John's eyes, the promise of indestructible peace was no sentimental tonic for despondency, but a factor that helped to shape history, vital equipment for a century of tension and peril, an inner invincibility that ensured the church's survival and final victory.

3. *"I have overcome."* What a superb last word — "Courage, I have overcome"! The whole atmosphere in the upper room has now changed, and so has Jesus' mood. The facts remain as they were, but in new light, transfigured by Jesus' faith. The hostility that awaits them is but the last fury of a beaten foe; the enemy's last throe will overthrow himself; the world will overreach its own intention, and by judging Jesus judge itself. Evil stands forever condemned by what it did to Jesus, and all remaining struggle, resistance, and conflict, constitute only "mopping-up operations" following decisive victory. Of the final outcome there is no question:

> O love of God, O sin of man,
> In this dread act your strength is tried,
> And victory remains with love —
> For he, our Lord, is crucified.

(F. W. Faber [1814–1863], "O Come and Mourn with Me a While")

A perceptive verse! Christ, by dying, has overcome: deliverance would have been defeat.

But we must be clear what such victory means. In part, it lay in Christ's refusal to render evil for evil, spite for spitefulness, revenge threatened for violence suffered. Jesus refused to be beaten to the level of the world and its methods. His unconquerable spirit remained unsullied to the end: as he had earlier said, "the ruler of this world is coming. He has no power over me. . . ." That is victory.

In part, too, Christ's victory lay in showing that such resistance to evil can be sustained; that the world can be beaten in spite of all appearances; that in the faithful soul truth is tougher than falsehood, love outlasts hatred, goodness is stronger than evil, and life defeats death.

But most of all, Christ's victory lay in the actual breaking of the power of evil that held men and women captive, loosening its grip upon countless human hearts, minds, wills, and imaginations. By his death, as the whole history of the church has shown, Jesus liberated many from fear, subjection, slavery, superstition, ignorance of God, and love of evil. Every redeemed soul witnesses to that vicarious victory — vicarious, yet shared. Every Christian who has faced death calmly, and died nobly, witnesses to the same effect. And all the millions who through the gospel, in the twentieth century no less than in all the intervening ages, have been set free from the terror of evil spirits and demonic power loudly proclaim that victory.

Indeed, whenever the Christian sings the goodness of creation, the glory of the world, the joy of life —

> All creatures of our God and King,
> Lift up your voice and with us sing
>> Hallelujah!
> Thou burning sun with golden beam,
> Thou silver moon with softer gleam . . .
>
> Thou rushing wind that art so strong,
> Ye clouds that sail in heaven along,
> Thou rising morn — in praise rejoice:
> Ye lights of evening, find a voice . . .
>
> Thou flowing water, pure and clear,
> Make music for thy Lord to hear,
> Thou fire so masterful and bright
> That givest man both warmth and light . . .
>
> Dear mother earth . . .
>> O praise him, hallelujah!
>>> (St. Francis of Assisi [1182–1226],
>>> trans. W. H. Draper [1855–1933])

117

—he rarely understands that he is celebrating the marvellous change Christ wrought in the deepest human consciousness. For Jesus created the strong conviction, almost entirely unknown in the ancient world, that the universe is no menacing haunt of ghosts, hobgoblins, demons, fate, and mystic powers of evil, but *friendly*. He persuaded men again that the earth is the Lord's, not Satan's—the Lord's, who loved man and wished him well. The long-dreaded "prince of darkness," the "ruler of this world," was put down, and so effectively that generations of Christians have simply ceased to believe in him!

So far-reaching was the victory of Christ at Calvary—over the world and its ways, over sin and evil, over all that opposed his Father's will, over death and the fear of death. By demonstrating God's love, and his own love, in redeeming grace, Jesus opened the prison-house of superstitious fear, lifted the burden of guilt and uncleanness, and set men and women free to enjoy his Father's creation. "*Be of good cheer*" is the final word of the discourse, for "I have overcome the world."

So as the long conversation ends, the gloom and foreboding in that chamber besieged by fears lift and brighten. A gleam of approaching victory flashes among the shadows, a gleam that shall gather strength to break in radiant splendor from an empty tomb on Easter morning.

And after prayer, Jesus strode forth to Calvary, not alone, his heart at peace, already triumphant.

> *So if ye will, sit down upon the ground,*
> *Yet not to weep and wail, but calmly look around.*
> *Whate'er befell,*
> *Earth is not hell:*
> *Now, too, as when it first began,*
> *Life is yet life, and man is man.*
> *For all that breathe beneath the heaven's high cope,*
> *Joy with grief mixes, with despondence hope.*
> *Hope conquers cowardice; joy, grief;*
> *Or at the least, faith conquers unbelief.*
> *Though dead, not dead,*
> *Not gone, though fled,*
> *Not lost, not vanished:*

In the great gospel and true creed
He is yet risen indeed;
  Christ is yet risen!
    (A. H. Clough [1819–1861], "Easter Day, Naples, 1849")

Lead ME, Lord, a willing captive, in the train of thy
   triumph.

Far-ranging Intercession

16:
The Lord's Prayer for Us

JOHN 17:1–26

When Jesus had spoken these words, he lifted up his eyes to heaven and said, "Father, the hour has come; glorify thy Son that the Son may glorify thee, since thou hast given him power over all flesh, to give eternal life to all whom thou hast given him. And this is eternal life, that they know thee the only true God, and Jesus Christ whom thou hast sent. I glorified thee on earth, having accomplished the work which thou gavest me to do; and now, Father, glorify thou me in thy own presence with the glory which I had with thee before the world was made.

"I have manifested thy name to the men whom thou gavest me out of the world; thine they were, and thou gavest them to me, and they have kept thy word. Now they know that everything that thou hast given me is from thee; for I have given them the words which thou gavest me, and they have received them and know in truth that I came from thee; and they have believed that thou didst send me. I am praying for them; I am not praying for the world but for those whom thou hast given me, for they are thine; all mine are thine, and thine are mine, and I am glorified in them. And now I am no more in the world, but they are in the world, and I am coming to thee. Holy Father, keep them in thy name which thou hast given me, that they may be one, even as we are one. While I was with them, I kept them in thy name which thou hast given me; I have guarded them, and none of them is lost but the son of perdition, that the scripture might be fulfilled. But now I am coming to thee; and these things I speak in the world, that they may have my joy fulfilled in themselves. I have given them thy word; and the world has hated them because they are not of the world, even as I am not of the world. I do not pray that thou shouldst take them out of the world but that thou shouldst keep them from the evil one. They are not of the world, even as I am not of the world. Sanctify them in the truth; thy word is truth. As thou didst send me into the world, so I have sent them into the world. And for their sake I consecrate myself, that they also may be consecrated in truth.

"I do not pray for these only, but also for those who are to believe in me through their word, that they may all be one; even as thou, Father, art in me, and I in thee, that they also may be in us, so that the world may believe that thou hast sent me. The glory which thou hast given me I have given to them, that they may be one even as we are one, I in them and thou in me, that they may become perfectly one, so that the world may know that thou hast sent me and hast loved them even as thou hast loved me. Father, I desire that they also, whom thou hast given me, may be with me where I am, to behold my glory which thou hast given me in thy love for me before the foundation of the world. O righteous Father, the world has not known thee, but I have known thee; and these know that thou hast sent me. I made known to them thy name, and I will make it known, that the love with which thou hast loved me may be in them, and I in them."

HERE, in chapter 17, we eavesdrop at the eternal throne; meditation must be more than usually reverent, and cautious.

Nothing remotely resembling this chapter is found elsewhere in Scripture. In all the Gospels, references abound to Jesus at prayer, and sometimes we are told what he prayed for or gave thanks for: but nowhere else is so full expression given in words to the intimate relation of Father and Son. Previous nights of prayer, or morning devotions, are recorded but veiled. Here we are permitted to listen, and to wonder.

The Nature of Our Lord's Praying

It is striking how clearly the Lord's own prayer and the "Lord's Prayer" given as pattern to the disciples bear the marks of the same mind. Each is addressed to the Father; where in the model prayer the phrase "which art in heaven" reminds us that our Father is also our God, in Jesus' prayer the epithets "holy" and "righteous" (vv. 11, 25) likewise temper intimacy with reverence. "Hallowed be thy name" is here echoed in four references to God's "name"; and in both prayers the divine will is kept paramount. A prayer for deliverance from evil occurs in both the pattern prayer and Jesus' prayer, while the "power" of God is here mentioned once, his "glory" seven times.

In both prayers, it is simply assumed that the Father will

hear our prayers, and that mature praying is always corporate, shared, intercessory, and never wholly individual. Also assumed is the contrast between the divine society ("thy kingdom," "those whom thou hast given me") and the "world." The desire that "as it is [now] in heaven so [let it be] on earth" is the heart of both prayers. These are remarkable parallels.

Yet John 17 is *not* a meditation on "the Lord's Prayer," for the differences are even more remarkable. In Christ's own prayer there is no petition for forgiveness, or to be kept from temptation, or even any thought of progress to be attained or new surrender to be made. Jesus prays, as he has been speaking, out of the profoundest sense of perfect unity with the Father. The previous conversation moved from "He who has seen me has seen the Father" to "I am not alone, for the Father is with me." The Lord's praying is but this essential unity made articulate, that the disciples and (through John) the church in all generations may overhear.

The phrasing of the prayer, if not so familiar to us, would be startling.

> Father, the hour has come; glorify thy Son that the Son may glorify thee, since thou hast given him power over all flesh. . . . Father, glorify thou me in thy own presence with the glory which I had with thee before the world was made. . . . thou didst send me. . . . I am coming to thee. . . . we are one. . . . as thou, Father, art in me, and I in thee, that they also may be in us. . . . I in them and thou in me. . . .

No disciple ever prayed like that, or ever will.

Jesus' praying is different also in tone. On one side, Jesus meditates upon his ministry, now completed, and offers it to the Father for acceptance as fulfillment of the mission on which he had been sent.

> I glorified thee on earth, having accomplished the work which thou gavest me to do. . . . I have manifested thy name. . . . I have given them the words which thou gavest me. . . . Now I am no more in the world. . . .

It is this aspect of the prayer that earns the description "Prayer of Consecration," especially in view of the words, "For their sake I consecrate myself" (v. 19). The title hardly applies to the whole prayer.

On the other side, the tone rises to a personal initiative and an expression of *will*:

Now, Father, glorify thou me. . . . I am coming to thee. . . . I do not pray that thou shouldst take them out of the world . . . keep them. . . . I do not pray for these only. . . . the world has not known thee, but I have known thee. . . . I will make [thy name] known. . . .

The strongest expression of this tone of personal will is much debated. "Father, I desire . . ." (v. 24) in the newer versions appears in older translations as "Father, I will. . . ." It is perhaps enough to notice the unexpected use in prayer of any expression that could (and in Greek usage certainly often does) bear the more assertive translation, "I will." No disciple ever dared to pray in that tone.

This is probably the clue to the real purpose of this chapter within John's Gospel, as the offering of Jesus' ministry, and his men, to God. This recognition prompts another title, "the High Priestly Prayer," as though John 17 anticipates the continuing intercessory ministry of Jesus during the time between his "going" and his "coming." The words "I am no more in the world" suggest such anticipation, and the whole thought is attractive.

Nevertheless, John does not explicitly say all this, nor does he anywhere use for Jesus the high priestly language that Hebrews uses; "advocate" (1 John 2:1) is a near thought, but not the same. More probably, John inserts the prayer as a final illustration of that subordination and dependence on the Father (here recalled in the Father's "gift" of the men, the word, the name, and the glory), which in Jesus was combined with intimacy, perfect knowledge, and complete unity. The prayer is "Christology made articulate," the divine interrelationship being revealed in the only way that human hearts could understand it — total confidence uttered in speech and breathed into prayer.

John's record of this evening opened with the most solemn reminder that the Father had given all things into Jesus' hands, who "came from God and went to God"; it closes with that majestic reality finding utterance in adoration, thanksgiving, petition, and intercession that almost outrun thought. To the end, the Servant remains the perfect, transparent vehicle of the Father's mind and will, his love and purpose. The nature of Christ's

125

praying is entirely appropriate to his own nature as eternal Servant-Son.

The Range of the Lord's Praying

1. *Jesus prays that his life-work shall be crowned with true success.* The language is unexpected, but appropriate: Christ's whole ministry is summed up in the words "I glorified thee on earth, having accomplished the work which thou gavest me to do." Behind that ministry lay the glory of Christ's original commission: "Glorify thy Son . . . since thou hast given him power over all flesh, to give eternal life to all whom thou hast given him." The only "glory" in which the Son rejoices is that of imparting life. (The definition of eternal life [v. 3] is unexpected in prayer, and together with the formal name "Jesus Christ" for "me" reads more like a comment by the writer than a petition of Jesus. Just possibly, it is a phrase that has crept into early manuscripts when the passage was used in worship. Certainly, to know the true God through the true, historical Christ is for John the secret of eternal life: the words sound like his.)

Behind both ministry and commission lay yet further "glory," the original, native glory of the only-begotten Son — "the glory which I had with thee before the world was made." It is this glory, in God's "own presence," which Jesus prays shall be restored (v. 5). But "glorify thou me" must be understood as John has used such a phrase throughout his Gospel. (We must recall again that in chapter 7, Christ was "not yet glorified"; in 12, "the hour" had "come for the Son of man to be glorified," and he immediately explains his death; in 13, as Judas leaves the upper room to set in motion the process of betrayal, Jesus said, "Now is the Son of man glorified, and in him *God is glorified.* . . . Yet a little while I am with you. . . .")

The Father's glory, which it is the Servant's joy to promote, the Son's glory, which he surrendered and would now resume, and the coming death-resurrection-ascension are elements in one total event — the mission, ministry, and passion by which God's purpose will be achieved. Here, therefore, "glorify thou me," like "glorify thy name" in chapter 12, expresses Christ's deliberate acceptance of the remaining work, the passion, as the path to the fulfillment of his mission and to the glory that waits beyond the cross.

For that perfect consummation of God's plan Jesus now prays, and that is *all* that Jesus will ask, by way of personal petition, in the whole prayer. The request is not that he shall be spared, that "the cup shall pass from him," but that the purpose of his coming shall be fulfilled and the Father glorified.

John testifies that the prayer was granted. Looking back upon the Christ-event, he saw it transfigured with unearthly splendor. Where some Christians were looking heavenward anticipating some glory in Jesus that had not yet been revealed, John declares roundly, "We *have* beheld his glory . . ." (1:14). Christ will come again, but Christian eyes will never see greater "glory" than shone in that earthly ministry, in the radiance of the cross, and through the doorway of the open tomb. His prayer was granted.

2. *Jesus prays, especially and at length, for the Eleven.* The Master's *description* of his men as he lifts them to God in prayer is very remarkable. Although they formed the nucleus of the church, with the leaders of coming years already among them, it would be wrong to confine these verses to apostles then, or to "ministers" today—except, perhaps, to acknowledge that Christ's gracious words apply to us in proportion to the effort we make, the responsibility we carry, in his service.

> I have manifested thy name [that is, thy true nature] to the men . . . they have kept thy word. . . . they know that everything that thou hast given me is from thee; for I have given them the words which thou gavest me; and they have received them and know in truth that I came from thee; and they have believed that thou didst send me. . . . these know that thou hast sent me. I made known to them thy name. . . . Thou hast loved them. . . .

Such things are true of every Christian: reception and retention of Christ's word, recognition of the divine source of Christ's power and mission. Nothing is said of their especial saintliness or qualifications: all is privilege, opportunity, and gift. The description continues:

> All whom thou hast given. . . . the men whom thou gavest me. . . . thine they were, and thou gavest them to me. . . . those whom thou hast given me . . . they are thine; all mine are thine, and thine are mine, and I am glorified in them.

127

> ... keep them in thy name which thou has given me. ... I kept them in thy name which thou hast given me ... none of them is lost but the son of perdition, that the scripture might be fulfilled. ... I desire that they also, whom thou hast given me, may be with me. ...

The emphasis is unmistakable. The disciples are the Father's gift to the Son: as a comfort — "I am glorified in them," though vilified among all others; and as a trust — "Thou gavest them me. ... None of them is lost. ... I have kept them."

No less remarkable is the Master's *ministry* toward his men.

> I have manifested thy name to the men. ... I have given them the words thou gavest. ... While I was with them, I kept them ... I have guarded them. ... The glory which thou hast given me I have given to them. ... I made known to them thy name. ...

One senses the bond of concern mingled with affection and trust that bound the lonely Jesus to his "friends," though they had so much to learn. Now, as continued expression of that concern, Jesus prays for the Eleven, with realism and understanding.

Realistically, Jesus delineates the disciples' position in the world. Their experience has effectively separated them from the rest of men: they are "out of the world" (v. 6), "not of the world" (v. 14, repeated v. 16). The distinction is radical — Christ is not praying for the world (v. 9), for there are things one cannot ask for unbelievers; "the only hope for the world is that it cease to be the world." Being thus different, the disciples are exposed to the world's envy and hatred.

Yet those so separated from the world by faith and experience are nevertheless not set apart in aloofness, indifference, contempt, or irresponsibility; they are sent back into the world. They remain in the world as he comes to the Father (v. 11). Jesus does not pray that they will be taken out of the world, as by some premature "rapture" or some world-denying withdrawal into hermitage or monastery, for that would defeat the purpose of their calling.

At point after point Jesus compares the disciples' situation with his own. Repetition underlines this: "they are not of the world even as I am not of the world" (vv. 14 *and* 16); "as thou didst send me into the world, so I have sent them into the world";

"I consecrate myself, that they also may be consecrated. . . ." The separation from the world, the mission to the world, the self-dedication to God for the world's sake, the role of Servant of God within the world are all his first, and then theirs because they are his men. That states their future situation without sentiment and without pretence.

But Christ's realism is matched by sympathetic understanding. The reiterated burden of his prayer is that they shall be *kept* (vv. 11, 15; "I kept . . . I guarded . . .," v. 12; "sanctify them" means "keep them for divine use," v. 17). "I pray that thou shouldst keep them from the evil one": the pressures of the world toward evil would be more menacing even than its physical perils, as John and his contemporaries well knew. The loss of "the son of perdition," now mentioned for the last time in this interview, is a solemn warning that even the most privileged experience with Jesus is no permanent safeguard in itself.

But they are God's, and Christ's (v. 10), though henceforth without his visible guardianship (v. 11). He had kept them "in God's name" (v. 12) — here, almost a fortress in which souls may hide in evil days, a breastplate of divine protection when the world's hostility runs high. By the time John wrote, it was possible to testify that this prayer, too, had been granted: "We know that any one born of God does not sin, but He who was born of God keeps him and the evil one does not touch him."

"Keep them . . . that they may be one, even as we are one" (v. 11; cf. 22); "that they may become perfectly one, so that the world may know that thou hast sent me" (v. 23). At the close of the evening Christ's thought returns to the appeal for mutual loyalty before the persecuting world, and that would impress the world, the appeal that rose to his lips as Judas left. But now he sets an even higher standard, "as we are one." Of course this is no mere unified organization, no uniformity of liturgical custom or dogmatic system: it is a gross misuse of Jesus' prayer to make of it propaganda for church politics. The unity between Father and Son is unity of life, of purpose, and of love: that is far deeper, more enduring, and for us more difficult to achieve even than well-oiled ecclesiastical engineering.

That is why, in addition to the higher standard, Jesus adds to his command his personal prayer. Only by God's help would such mutual loyalty be preserved, such spiritual oneness endure, grow, and become complete (v. 23). It takes God to keep the church together, even yet.

In their preservation from evil and division would lie the disciples' "consecration" for the work to which they were appointed; while in that moral strength and deepening fellowship would be preserved the joy that would lend radiance to their witness (v. 13).

"Keep them" . . . "unite them" . . . "consecrate them" . . . "give them joy" — how desperately the church still needs the intercession of Jesus!

3. *Jesus prays, explicitly, for the church that is to be* — in fact, for us. The word "church" is not used, but there is no doubt that it is the ever-widening fellowship of believing people, such as John knew, that was in Christ's thought. "I do not pray for these only, but also for those who are to believe in me through their word. . . ." The Eleven are not only the nucleus of the church, but the agents through whose witness it will come into existence.

The "church" has appeared already in John's Gospel as the children of God scattered abroad whom Christ would gather into one (11:52); it will appear again in the beatitude pronounced upon those who, though they do not see Jesus, yet believe (20:29). Here, the church of all generations to the end of time is held before God through the intercession of its Head and Savior, even as in Revelation he stands among the churches clad in the vestments of the High Priest. As Paul says, Christ nourishes his church and cherishes it: that alone explains the invincible perseverance of the saints.

What Jesus asks for this wider circle includes again the unity created by mutual indwelling of Father, Son, and believers (v. 21). Jesus refers also to a share in "glory," already sampled in the gleam of splendor and light of hope brought into the lives of the Eleven (v. 22). He asks, too, for these distant believers who missed his day, that they might know true fellowship with him, in glory and in eternal love (vv. 24, 26).

Yet further, Jesus asks that all present and future disciples, who have known him in humiliation and followed him in eclipse, might at the last see his glory, and so realize the ultimate triumph of that love which issued from within the godhead in eternity past (v. 24) and sweeps forward to embrace them for eternity to come (v. 26). For hearts that love him, that will be reward enough.

John had seen how such unity and hope had sustained the church through bitter years; he had learned, too, that only when she spoke in unity and hope could the church witness convincingly before a skeptical world (vv. 21, 23). The world can recognize the divine mission of Christ and the love which prompted it only in the miracle of the church.

Up to this point in the whole discourse and prayer, "the world" has been only hostile, an evil system to keep separate from, to be convicted, to be feared and guarded against, and to overcome. Now the need of the world itself to hear and to believe in the mission of Christ and the love of God is brought into focus. The purpose of that mission is to reconcile, and the nature of that love is to create unity; the world can comprehend their meaning and feel their power only when it sees the message demonstrated in the ingathering of all races, classes, and types into a real fellowship of believers. A divided church cannot hope to reconcile a divided world; and the winning of that world is still God's purpose, Christ's mission, and the church's task.

The concluding verses of the Lord's prayer are in John's Gospel the last words of Jesus in private before his death. They form a solemn review and comment, wistful and yet bold, on the situation at the close of his ministry.

> O righteous Father, the world has not known thee, but I have known thee; and these have known that thou hast sent me. I made known to them thy name, and I will make it known, that the love with which thou hast loved me may be in them, and I in them.

The failure of the public ministry, in the sense that the world still does not know the Father, is the overall circumstance governing the future. Believers, from the beginning, are set within an environment of unbelief.

There is something tentative, too, in the affirmation concerning the disciples. They have known that God sent Christ, and something of the true character ("the name") of God. They will know more as Christ, by the Spirit, leads them into further truth: that note of progress still to be made is sounded again

131

(v. 26). Jesus does not assume in them perfect knowledge or understanding; they remain disciple-learners, pilgrims of the true and living way. Yet what they do know rests on his divine authority, is certain so far as it goes, and goes far enough to save.

But in the end, more certain and more important than knowledge is love. Christ's thought ends where it began, with the love with which God so loved the world, now loving the disciples, as the Father loves the Son.

According to Matthew, the final promise of Jesus to his church was, "Lo, I am with you always, to the close of the age." According to John, the same assurance is given more tersely: "I in them." Perhaps this is all the more moving in that it is spoken just before Jesus steps forth to cross the brook Kidron, into the garden and on to the cross.

The situation, then, is perilous; the world antagonistic and unbelieving; the future dark for Master and men: all this is accepted without resentment, without fear. Jesus goes forward; his men, soon to be scattered and shaken, will also in time go forward, embued with the Spirit, united in loyalty, sure of God's love in Christ, with the gleam of glory in their hearts, and aware of the unfailing presence of the living Christ among them. In them, and upon us, the Lord's own prayer is being constantly fulfilled.

> *O Thou, the contrite sinner's Friend,*
> *Who, loving, lovest to the end,*
> *On this alone my hopes depend,*
>   *That Thou wilt plead for me.*
>
> *When, weary in the Christian race,*
> *Far off appears my resting-place,*
> *And, fainting, I mistrust Thy grace,*
>   *Then, Saviour, plead for me.*
>
> *When I have erred and gone astray,*
> *Afar from Thine and wisdom's way,*
> *And see no glimmering, guiding ray,*
>   *Still, Saviour, plead for me.*

When Satan, by my sins made bold,
Strives from Thy cross to loose my hold,
Then with Thy pitying arms enfold,
And plead, oh, plead, for me.

When the full light of heavenly day
Reveals my sins in dread array,
Say, Thou hast washed them all away;
Dear Saviour, plead for me.

(Charlotte Elliott [1789–1871])